Selected

Graphic Design from Europe

B

ABCDEFGHIJKLMNÑOPQRSTUVWXYZ
abcdefghijklmnñopqrstuvwxyz
0123456789!?,"¢$&%[ ]*

Typography: Bodoni
Designer: Giambattista Bodoni
Year: 1798

Selected B.
Publisher: Index Book, S.L.

Consell de Cent 160 local 3
08015 Barcelona.
Tel: +34 93 454 55 47
Fax: + 34 93 454 84 38
Email: ib@indexbook.com
http://www.indexbook.com

Design: artima˜a
Editorial coordinator: Neus Bas, Federica Sala
New media coordinator: Wenceslao Sanz
Selection day photographs: Estibaliz Soto
Text Edition: Kristen Short

ISBN 978-84-92643-95-0

Printed in China

Selected

Graphic Design from **Europe**

B

Sylvie Estrada

Publisher, Index Book

This is the second year that we are presenting Selected. The reason for our return is the positive reception aroused by the first edition, Selected A. The aim of this project from our publishing house is to show the measure of creativity generated in Europe during the past year.

Although it is a small-format book, we thought it essential to devote a double page to each work so that each artist has his/her own individual space in our project. We offer in like fashion two volumes, one dedicated to professionals and the other to schools. With this division we aim to present an opportunity to the youngest designers so that new emerging talent can become known.

Lastly, just to emphasize, we are going forward in the hope that the route we have chosen is the right one, since, even though the experience from last year suggests that it is, our objective continues to be to consolidate this project.

Schools

The Judges

Frank Philippin, Inge Gobert.

First of all we would like to say how much fun it is to judge and select good student work! At its best, student work is fresh, uncompromising, innocent and a potent expression of each generation. At its very best, it is often better and more refreshing than professional work, because of the spirit in which it is made and the freedom that students cut out for themselves. These qualities were most present in the editorial work of this year's entries, so we enjoyed judging this section the most. The other categories couldn't quite compete, mainly because of the amount of entries (students of this world, send your work!), but of course we still found work that was of a very high quality and stood out. We hope and wish that in the future the student part of Selected will grow and grow, as the Selected publications are truly inspiring books and produced with great respect for the work.
Secondly, we really enjoyed being part of the Selected judges and wish all the participants good luck for their future!

Inge Gobert & Frank Philippin

Index

Catalogues	12
Corporate Identity	30
Editorial	48
Exhibitions	104
Illustration	110
New Media	142
Packaging	158
Posters	168
Promotions	180
Typography	194
Directory	204

Catalogues

Design: Alexander Brade, Florian Renschke, Marijana Babic, Matthias Görlich, Rade Matic. **Title:** Show Down (publication). **Description:** 'Show Down' publication/catalogue (A1 size) accompanied the Show Down exhibition, describing and explaining all kind of conflicts in dictionary style (one side) and showing a famous soccer foul (other side). This publication accompanied the one-day exhibition at the University of Applied Sciences, Faculty of Design of Darmstadt. **School:** University of Applied Sciences Darmstadt. **Country:** Germany.

Design: Ana Araújo. **Title:** Anita Stencil Embroidery. **Description:** These pieces were based on the traditional Portuguese embroidery *Bordados*, but went beyond the original *Bordados* application and were used instead as a new street art style, something that has never been done or seen before. This catalogue was a college project divided in the following parts: What Is Portuguese Embroidery; How This Idea Occurred; Ways to Develop It; Graphic Identity; and finally, How to Exhibit It in the Streets. The pieces on this catalogue are unique, created through stencil technique and also incorporating stickers, with the objective of being applied and used on the streets, reinventing and exploring once more the thematic of street art. **School:** Escola Superior de Artes e Design de Caldas da Rainha. **Country:** Portugal.

Design: Joany Anthonio. **Title:** Spaces that ostensibly stay the same change with. **Description:** 'Spaces that ostensibly stay the same change with' is a book about the photographical experience of the city. The text and different ways of ranking the images constantly give the reader another perspective on the images. When you read the index, you will figure out that the whole content of the book is about Rotterdam. **School:** Willem de Kooning Academy. **Country:** The Netherlands.

004
005
Het oude gebouw van het Departement van Financien aan de Pietermaaiweg, staat nu te wachten op restauratie als monument, na eerst ook dienst te hebben gedaan als schoolgebouw voor I.F.E. (Instituto pa Formashon den Enfermeria - verpleegsters-opleiding). De nieuwe kantoren van Financien zijn per 2007 gehuisvest in het oude ABN bankgebouw aan de overkant van het oude monumentale onderkomen.
175
002
005
017
028
051
085
099
112
124
134
Flamingo's zijn roze door het voedsel dat ze eten, voornamelijk garnalen en andere kreeftachtigen. In deze garnaaltjes zit de kleurstof caroteen en deze kleurstof wordt tijdens de groei van nieuwe veren opgenomen in de veer.
175
005
048
080
107
137
143
149
155
161
169

036
037

Design: Loes Hilhorst. **Title:** ANS – Algemeen Nederlands Schrift. **Description:** The *'Algemeen Nederlands Schrift'* or Common Dutch Script has been shaped from a compilation of 100 hand writings from the Dutch population. This guide for designers, typographers and others interested shows how one can develop new typographic families out of the richness of the Common Dutch Script. **School:** Willem de Kooning Academy. **Country:** The Netherlands.

Nederland
heeft
16 577 612
unieke
handschriften

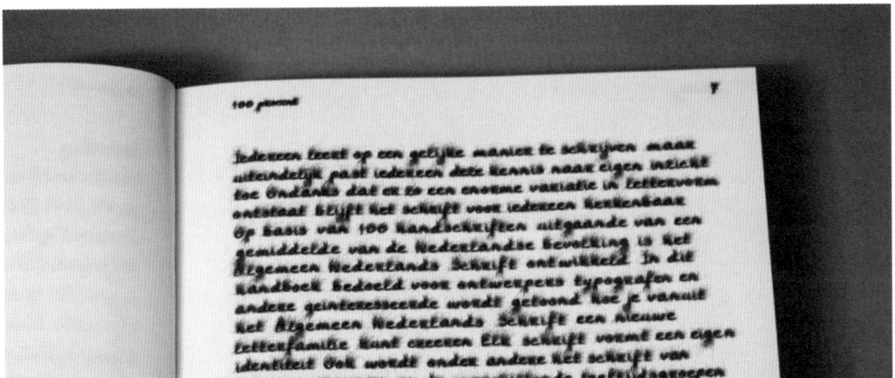
Iedereen leert op een gelijke manier te schrijven maar
uiteindelijk past iedereen deze kennis naar eigen inzicht
toe Ondanks dat er zo een enorme variatie in lettervorm
ontstaat blijft het schrift voor iedereen herkenbaar
Op basis van 100 handschriften uitgaande van een
gemiddelde van de Nederlandse bevolking is het
Algemeen Nederlands Schrift ontwikkeld In dit
handboek bedoeld voor ontwerpers typografen en
andere geinteresseerde wordt getoond hoe je vanuit
het Algemeen Nederlands Schrift een nieuwe
letterfamilie kunt creeren Elk schrift vormt een eigen
identiteit Ook wordt onder andere het schrift van
mannen vrouwen en de verschillende leeftijdsgroepen
uitgelicht Naast deze categorieen zijn er nog vele
mogelijkheden om de letterfamilie uit te breiden
Met dit schrift kun je verschillende doelgroepen
hun eigen typografische identiteit geven

Design: Lola Tinnirello. **Title:** Graphic story. **Description:** The general topic and starting point of this little book is about copy and paste, specifically about clichés, stereotypes and how they are growing. After research and reflection, it became clear that most of these originate in society, education, media. In this way, human beings are conditioned from their childhoods. So I asked myself why it has to be like this way since I didn't choose these ideas and assumptions that were conveyed to me; I just received and accepted them. Why did I accept these and what are my opinions now? I chose to create my own story, one in which I mix, copy and transform reality, perturbing usual social norms. **School:** IADE – Creative University (Escola Superior de Design). **Country:** Portugal.

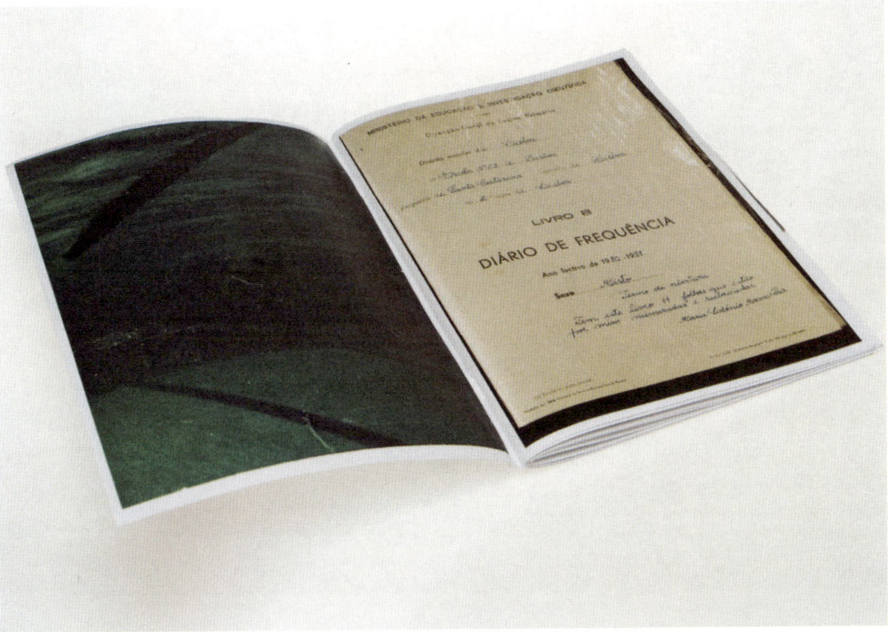
LIVRO B
DIÁRIO DE FREQUÊNCIA

NOBODY
KNOWS
WhAt
i'm
WORTH

SCHIETPARTIJ OP DAM!
KNAL TIJDENS DODEN-HERDENKING DAM
DODEN-HERDENKING OP DAM VERSTOORD
DODEN-HERDENKING OP DE SECONDE
PANIEK BIJ DODEN-HERDENKING
VIER MILJOEN KIJKERS ZIEN CHAOS BIJ
63 GEWONDEN DOOR PANIEK TIJDENS DODEN-HERDENKING

DODEN-HERDENKING DAM
PANIEK BIJ 2 MINUTEN STILTE A'DAM
DODEN-HERDENKING OP DAM VERSTOORD
VIER MILJOEN KIJKERS ZIEN CHAOS BIJ
PREMIER: POGING HERDENKING TE VERSTOREN
BALKENENDE: VERSTORING HERDENKING WAS BEWUSTE ACTIE
VERSTORING DODEN-HERDENKING DOOR INCIDENT
BREAKING NEWS: DODENHERDENKING VERSTOORD DOOR ONBEKENDE MAN
PANIEK BIJ DODEN-HERDENKING
PANIEK OP DE DAM TIJDENS DODEN-HERDENKING
MENSEN-MASSA IN PANIEK TIJDENS HERDENKING OP DE DAM
BEVRIJDINGS-DAG AMSTERDAM GAAT GEWOON DOOR
VERSTORING DODEN-HERDENKING AAN-GEKONDIGD
INCIDENT DODEN-HERDENKING NIET VAN INVLOED OP BEVRIJDINGS-DAG

Design: Miriam Thijssen. **Title:** Damschreeuwer weer vrij. **Description:** The subject of the book *'Damschreeuwer weer vrij'* is the news item of the screaming man who briefly disrupted the Remembrance of the Dead at Damsquare in Amsterdam. The pattern of screaming mouths not only represents the screaming itself, but is also a metaphor for the speed in which news travels. **School:** Willem de Kooning Academy. **Country:** The Netherlands.

Design: Neus Bayarri. **Title:** Martín López Lam. Todo lo que dicen de lo nuestro es mentira. **Description:** This catalogue of the artist Martín López Lam's works, halfway between fanzine and the book, translates the author's graphic style into an editorial format. The layout is thought to give a better perspective of each work. Typography is used as illustration, as the artist does. For the cover I've used linoleum cut, so each book is unique. **School:** Escuela de Arte y Superior de Diseño de Valencia. **Country:** Spain.

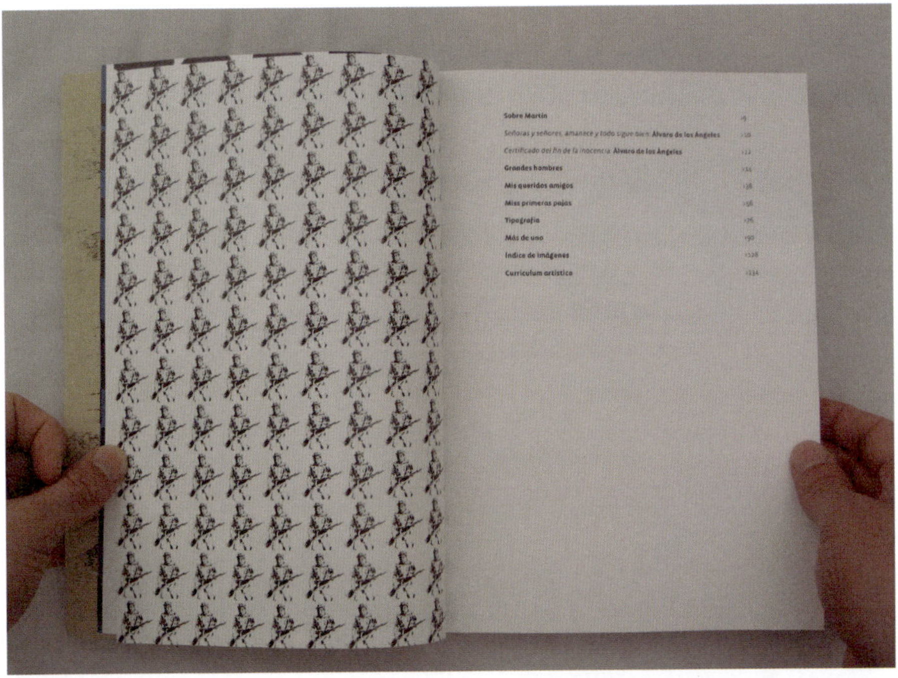
Sobre Martín
Señoras y señores, amanece y todo sigue bien. Álvaro de los Ángeles
Certificado del fin de la inocencia. Álvaro de los Ángeles
Grandes hombres
Mis queridos amigos
Miss primeras pajas
Tipografía
Más de uno
Índice de imágenes
Curriculum artístico

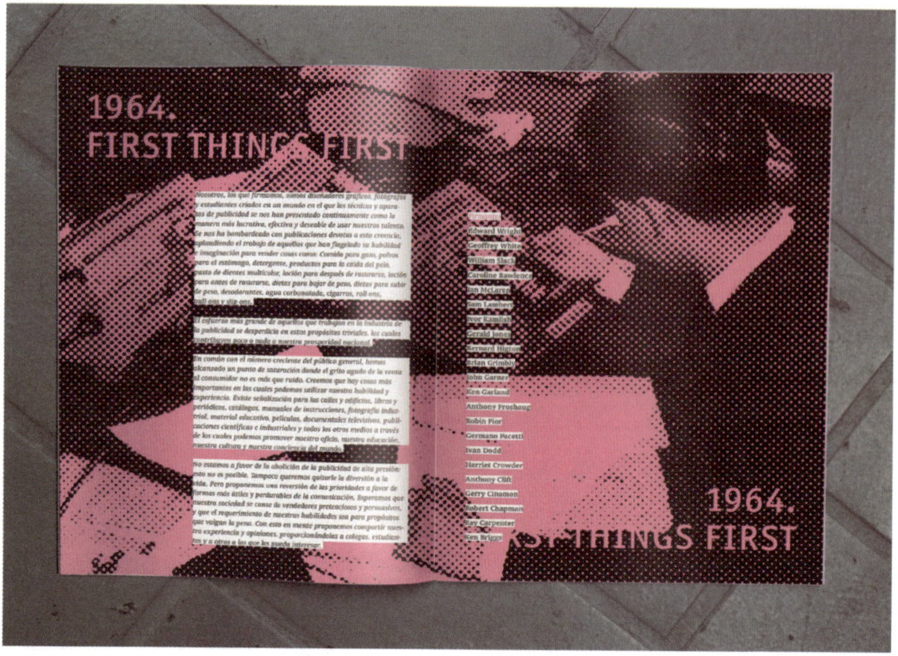

1964.
FIRST THINGS FIRST

Nosotros, los que firmamos, somos diseñadores gráficos, fotógrafos y estudiantes criados en un mundo en el que las técnicas y aparatos de publicidad se nos han presentado continuamente como la manera más lucrativa, efectiva y deseable de usar nuestros talento. Se nos ha bombardeado con publicaciones devotas a esta creencia, aplaudiendo el trabajo de aquellos que han flagelado su habilidad e imaginación para vender cosas como: Comida para gato, polvos para el estómago, detergente, productos para la caída del pelo, pasta de dientes multicolor, loción para después de rasurarse, loción para antes de rasurarse, dietas para bajar de peso, dietas para subir de peso, desodorantes, agua carbonatada, cigarros, roll-ons, pull-ons y slip-ons.

El esfuerzo más grande de aquellos que trabajan en la industria de la publicidad se desperdicia en estos propósitos triviales. los cuales contribuyen poco o nada a nuestra prosperidad nacional.

En común con el número creciente del público general, hemos alcanzado un punto de saturación donde el grito agudo de la venta al consumidor no es más que ruido. Creemos que hay cosas más importantes en las cuales podemos utilizar nuestra habilidad y experiencia. Existe señalización para las calles y edificios, libros y periódicos, catálogos, manuales de instrucciones, fotografía industrial, material educativo, películas, documentales televisivos, publicaciones científicas e industriales y todos los otros medios a través de los cuales podemos promover nuestro oficio, nuestra educación, nuestra cultura y nuestra conciencia del mundo.

No estamos a favor de la abolición de la publicidad de alta presión: esto no es posible. Tampoco queremos quitarle la diversión a la vida. Pero proponemos una reversión de las prioridades a favor de formas más útiles y perdurables de la comunicación. Esperamos que nuestra sociedad se canse de vendedores pretenciosos y persuasivos, y que el requerimiento de nuestras habilidades sea para propósitos que valgan la pena. Con esto en mente proponemos compartir nuestra experiencia y opiniones, proporcionándolas a colegas, estudiantes y a otros a los que les pueda interesar.

Firmantes
Edward Wright
Geoffrey White
William Slack
Caroline Rawlence
Ian McLaren
Sam Lambert
Ivor Kamlish
Gerald Jones
Bernard Higton
Brian Grimbly
John Garner
Ken Garland
Anthony Froshaug
Robin Fior
Germano Facetti
Ivan Dodd
Harriet Crowder
Anthony Clift
Gerry Cinamon
Robert Chapman
Ray Carpenter
Ken Briggs

1964.
FIRST THINGS FIRST

2000:
REACCIONES

Milton Glaser, conocido como uno de los mejores diseñadores gráficos de la historia además de ilustrador y profesor, aceptó firmar el manifiesto sólo después de que el boceto inicial fuera modificado, "era demasiado polémico y no lo suficientemente global, básicamente estaba de un lado, no había elasticidad en quien entraba a formar parte del juego. Era una especie de elige o muere. Lo que pienso sobre el tema en general, es que si tu no das a la gente un rumbo al que seguir, no te prestarán atención". A esto añadió: "Hay un área de ambigüedad sobre que es perjudicial y que no lo es. Estoy de acuerdo con el tema fundamental, que no es otro que uno debe de intentar no causar perjuicios".

Michael Bierut, presidente en aquella época de la AIGA y socio de la prestigiosa Pentagram, una empresa internacional de diseño ampliamente considerada por los diseñadores profesionales, hace distinción entre el marco del manifiesto en Adbusters, (una "vista muy absolutista del tipo, vende tu alma o haz arrodillarse al capitalismo") y su propia posición: es "más una invitación a cambiar las prioridades, que a repudiar completamente el trabajo comercial". A pesar de tener esta opinión, Bierut se alinea con muchos lectores contrarios al manifiesto debido a la naturaleza de los firmantes quienes entraban dentro del saco de los 'sospechoso habituales', personas contrarias al actual sistema político. En este contexto, estaba de acuerdo en que el propósito del manifiesto hubiera estado mejor presentado sin firmas.

Finalmente sugirió que "continua viéndose como una posición elitista y exclusivista, tomada por gente que puede permitirse el lujo de realizar lo que se relata en el manifiesto, opuesta a otros que han caído ante la tentación".

Jessica Helfand, en contraste con Glaser, sugirió que es "una llamada al orden, debe haber un entendimiento básico en el cual definamos los valores que llevamos a nuestro trabajo". A diferencia de Bierut, Helfand pensaba que el hecho de que firmaran los 'sospechosos habituales' fue uno de sus fuertes: "¿Hubiera obtenido tenido la misma repercurión si la hubieran firmado catorce mil personas (miembros de la IAGA)? Hubiera dejado de ser algo especial".

Stefan Sagmeister comentó que uno puede distinguir entre individuos para los que el "diseño juega un papel crucial en su vida" y para los que simplemente es una ocupación de nueve a cinco. A pesar de no firmar el manifiesto, Sagmeister dijo: "¿Por qué querría ser parte de esa increíble maquinaria que produce esta cantidad de increíble basura?", entendiendo 'basura' como el diseño mal concebido y ejecutado.

Gran parte de los retactores del manifiesto encuentran que detrás se esconde una campaña publicitaria anti-sistema contraria al capitalismo. Richard Wilde, comentó que el manifiesto era realmente ingenuo y altamente manipulado (posiblemente por Adbuster, revista perteneciente al entorno anti-sistema y de los 'culture jamming'). Defendió la publicidad apuntando que a pesar de lo que opinan muchos diseñadores, "las agencias estadounidenses contribuyen con el 10% de sus anuncios a temas sociales en la forma de Anuncios de Servicios Públicos (PSA)". Como respuesta indirecta a las palabras de Glaser recomendando a los diseñadores "no cometer perjuicios" Wilde dijo: "¿Quién puede decir que es bueno y que es malo? Desde donde estoy sentado puedo coger muchos productos y encontrar fallos reales".

Uno de los grandes defensores del manifiesto ha sido Media Foundation, a través de su publicación Adbusters. La revista, que históricamente ha fomentado una mezcla entre activismo medioambiental y de consumo, tiene pocos o ningún anuncio en su interior. De hecho, se ha hecho conocida por sus parodias a las campañas de publicidad más destacadas. Kate Lans, creó una agenda política que describió como 'culture jamming'. ››

Design: Víctor Arráez Abad. **Title:** First Things First Manifesto. **Description:** Publication researching and analyzing the 'First Things First Manifesto' in 1964 and 2000, including reactions, consequences, opinions and also an overview of several manifestos, pointing out similarities and differences between them. This project included a communication campaign using posters and flyers to spread the manifesto in addition to the main dossier. The goal was to make people think and reflect about today's design. **School:** Escuela de Arte y Superior de Diseño de Valencia. **Country:** Spain.

Corporate Identity

Design: Aljaz Vesel. **Title:** Project Boks. **Description:** Visual identity for 'Project Boks' – a student platform and art space, composed of two freight containers and redesigned into a white cube/black box. **School:** Academy of Fine Arts and Design. **Country:** Slovenia.

Avantgarde po avantgardah
razstava študentov slikarstva ALUO
Vljudno vabljeni na otvoritev razstave Avantgarde po avantgardah, ki bo v petek, 12. marca 2010, ob 20h v galeriji Boks.

AULA INICIACIÓN
AULA DESARROLLO
RECEPCIÓN
AULA APRENDIZAJE
DE 24 A 48 MESES

somos

Design: Cristóbal Sánchez Nicolás. **Title:** Somos. **Description:** *'Somos'* is a new concept of childhood gardens, areas based on simple shapes of the tangram. The graphic elements of the project represent the core communication of all applications made in the environment and in advertising, which features a minimalist colour palette. **School:** Escuela Superior de Diseño Región de Murcia. **Country:** Spain.

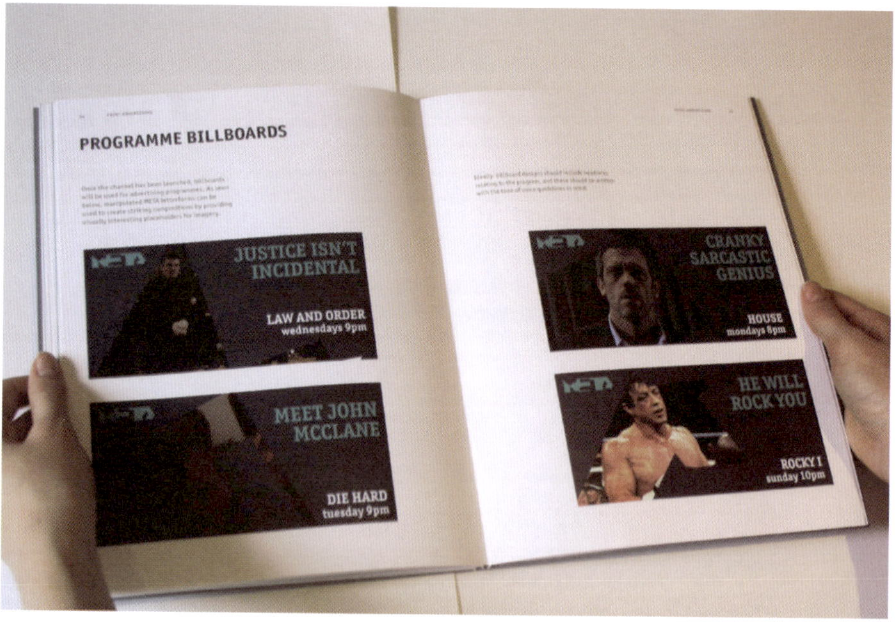
PROGRAMME BILLBOARDS
JUSTICE ISN'T INCIDENTAL
LAW AND ORDER
wednesdays 9pm
MEET JOHN MCCLANE
DIE HARD
tuesday 9pm
CRANKY SARCASTIC GENIUS
HOUSE
mondays 8pm
HE WILL ROCK YOU
ROCKY I
sunday 10pm

Design: Laura Andrews. **Title:** Meta TV. **Description:** The brief was to define and design an identity for a new TV channel: to build a big, bold brand; to forge emotional connections with the audiences; to be open and compelling; and above all, to be rooted in truth and effect. To carve out a place in people's hearts, to be challenging, and to express a clear point of view. The brand needs to be more than expected as the new TV channel is not just any other channel. The brand name chosen was Meta. The work shown is a 48-page book of brand guidelines, detailing the on-and-off air use of the identity. **School:** Nottingham Trent University. **Country:** United Kingdom.

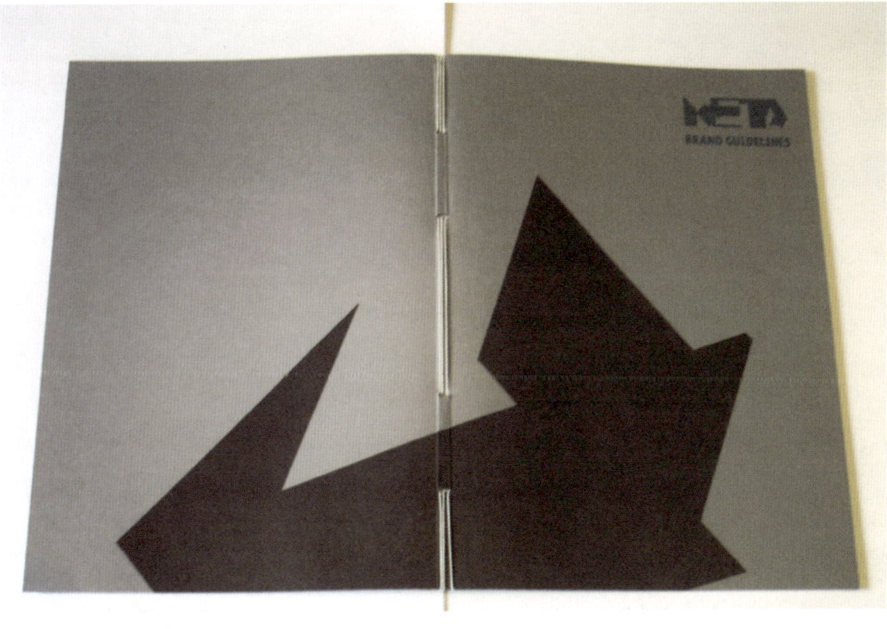

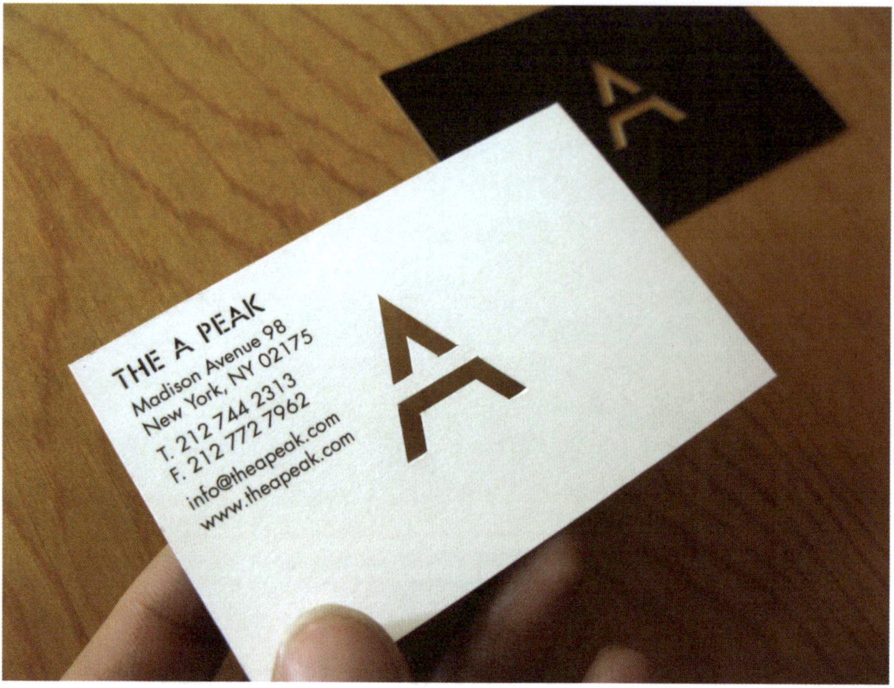

Design: Maggie Adrover. **Title:** THE A PEAK. **Description:** 'THE A PEAK' sells art. 'THE A PEAK' holds nighttime auctions in today's top fashion cities. 'THE A PEAK' sells works by the never-ending supply of emerging artists. 'THE A PEAK' is an unmistakably modern concentration of new trends in art. 'THE A PEAK' is a prestigious auction house like Sotheby's and Christie's. An elegant and timeless identity. An iconic firm, but one remaining invisible on the fringes of the works of art with which it coexists. Another development in terms of graphics that surround existing auction houses. **School:** Eina, Escola de Disseny i Art. **Country:** Spain.

THE A PEAK
THE AUCTION
26 · 11 · 10
AlexanderPlatz, 23
10178, Berlin
Germany
19:30 h. Vermissage
Auction, part I
Auction, part II
THE EXHIBITION

THE A PEAK
AUCTION NIGHT OF EMERGING ARTISTS
BERLIN 10
THE A PEAK

Design: Marc Pfaff and Johannes Schott. **Title:** mfg. – Museum für Gebrauch. **Description:** A radical proposal for renaming and rebranding Cologne's MAKK, a museum of applied arts with a growing focus on modern industrial design. The acronym 'mfg.' stands for the new name, *Museum für Gebrauch* (Museum of Use), but it is also the abbreviation for the phrase that typically ends a written conversation, *Mit freundlichen Grüßen* (with best regards). The imagery ironically explores the topic of use by depicting design classics in absurd contexts of utilization. **School:** Köln International School of Design. **Country:** Germany.

mfg.
AMORE
ETTORE

mfg.
DR. HERRMANN
KORTESHEIM
Direktor Restauration

Design: Marta Gualtero. **Title:** 'Bona Gana': A New Model of Social Dining Room. **Description:** Social dining rooms (what are called soup kitchens in the U.K. and other countries) do exist in our city, but they tend to be rather hidden and not widely known. They often do not have much in the way of resources and therefore, generally speaking, the food and service are not of very good quality. However, social dining rooms represent a service that is widely used and demand for it is gradually growing. Given this problem, *'Bona Gana'* proposes a social dining room, which, with its own visual identity, identifies and denounces a current reality in our city and offers a free meal in a quality setting. In order to survive, *'Bona Gana'* has a series of sponsors, private organisations from the gastronomy, hotel and catering industries. Using external communication, *'Bona Gana'* is able to offer these organisations advertising that is normally aimed at a well-to-do clientele with high purchasing power. The aim of *'Bona Gana'* is to call attention to the current state of social dining rooms, but at the same time show how actions can change them. Thanks to solidarity and communication, it is possible to create a dining room that, in addition to welcoming people without resources, offers a quality menu in a pleasant setting with a good service run by volunteers and social workers. **School:** Eina, Escola de Disseny i Art. **Country:** Spain.

BONA GANA
MENJADOR SOCIAL · 900 455 455 · BARCELONA · BONA GANA
4
FRUITA DEL TEMPS POMA
3
MACARRONS AMB TOMÀQUET I CARN
1
TOMAQUET XERRY AMB FORMATGE
2
ADVOCAT FARCIT DE GAMBES AMB SALSA

designaustria

DESIGN AWARD AWARDS 2010

Design: Martin Wunderer. **Title:** Design Award Awards. **Description:** 'Design Award Awards' is a detailed look at design awards. For graphic design alone, there are currently more than 100 awards, and their significance and quality are often difficult to assess for the designers themselves. In order to provide some orientation and guidance in the awards 'jungle' for myself and others, I developed Design Award Awards, an independent contest that confers awards for especially functional or innovative graphic design assessment systems. **School:** University of Applied Arts Vienna. **Country:** Austria.

borderline: flyer: front

Design: Wouter Medaer. **Title:** Logo as a System. **Description:** The name of the conference BORDERLINE was constantly changed to create anagrams – for example, NERDBOILER and ODER BERLIN. These different anagrams gave the conference a visibility and a representation of the term 'borderline'. The participants were asked to develop anagrams using their own names. The logo and corporate identity were designed as a system of anagrams (words) but also of images. **School:** MAD-Faculty. **Country:** Belgium.

cumulus
Design Guidelines
NERDBOILER
nightship
rides
gluten
movies
Filosofie
Fooi Liefs
'Pushing desing over the limit'
Anagram
Maanrag
pushing design over the limit
Pushing design
over the limit
NERDBOILER
NERDBOILER

Editorial

Bryan Edmond Mc Mullen
AGORAFOBIA
Mao Lee
COMPLEXES
Pierre Le Foullete
ANOREXIA
Diego Salazar
SOLEDAT

Design: Adrià Ventura. **Title:** Editorial de Psicología. **Description:** Cover and back cover design for publishing house that specialises in psychological texts. **School:** BAU, Escola Superior de Disseny. **Country:** Spain.

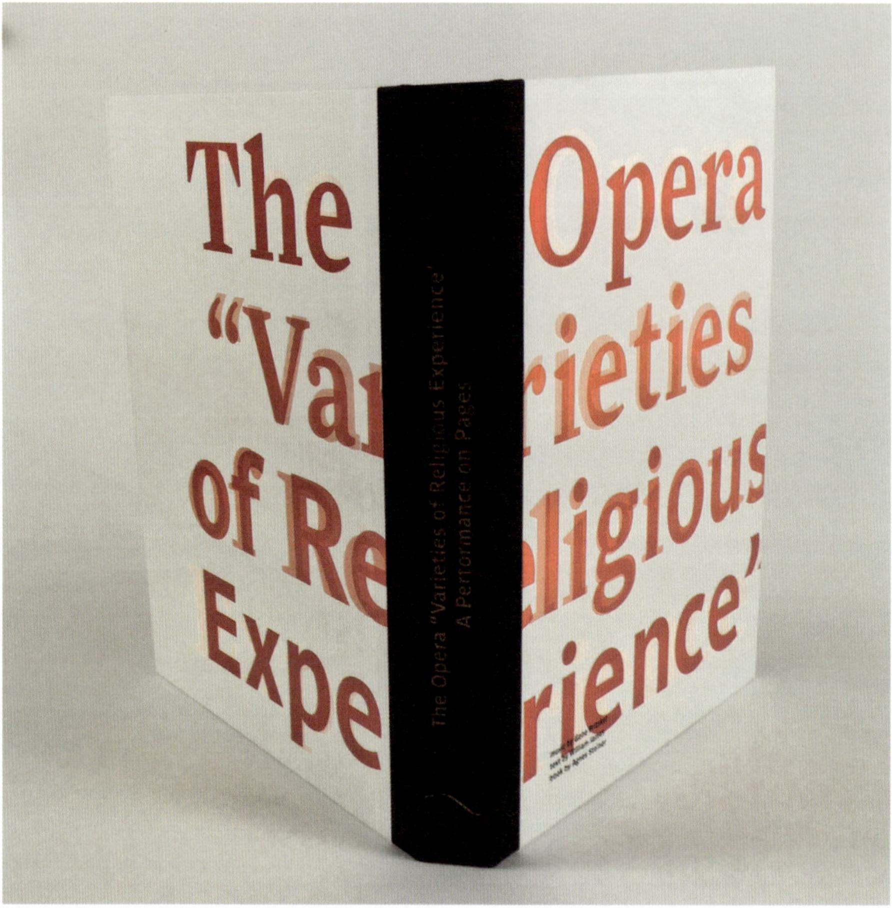

Design: Agnes Steiner. **Title:** The Opera 'Varieties of Religious Experience' – a Performance on Pages. **Description:** Based on the contemporary opera by the composer Gene Pritsker and the text of the philosopher William James, I created a new format featuring a dramaturgically treated, graphical visualization of the opera's music and its text, complementary to the existing *libretto*. This format allows the viewer and listener to experience a self-contained visual representation beyond the opera stage that both accompanies and complements the music. A *libretto* indicates a literary genre and also its medium. The new format's origin can be found in the subject's *libretto*, program and exclusive album artwork. The album package consists of two books, a map and the audio CD of the opera. The first book is made up of individual booklets, each issue matching the respective musical movement in the opera. The original scores are collected in a second book. A special navigation system connects the two books with each other, and the map gives a simple introduction to the opera's plot and to the relationships between the protagonists. It also serves as an overview of the content of the first book. Almost all photos of the visualization were produced with a digital pinhole camera, a reference to the discrepancy between the opera's contemporary music and the historical *libretto*. Basically the typographic concept takes up the main subject of the opera – the transcendental experience – in transforming the appearance of the text by gradually overlaying the two typefaces. It becomes the main visual key of the opera's media design. **School:** University of Applied Arts Vienna. **Country:** Austria.

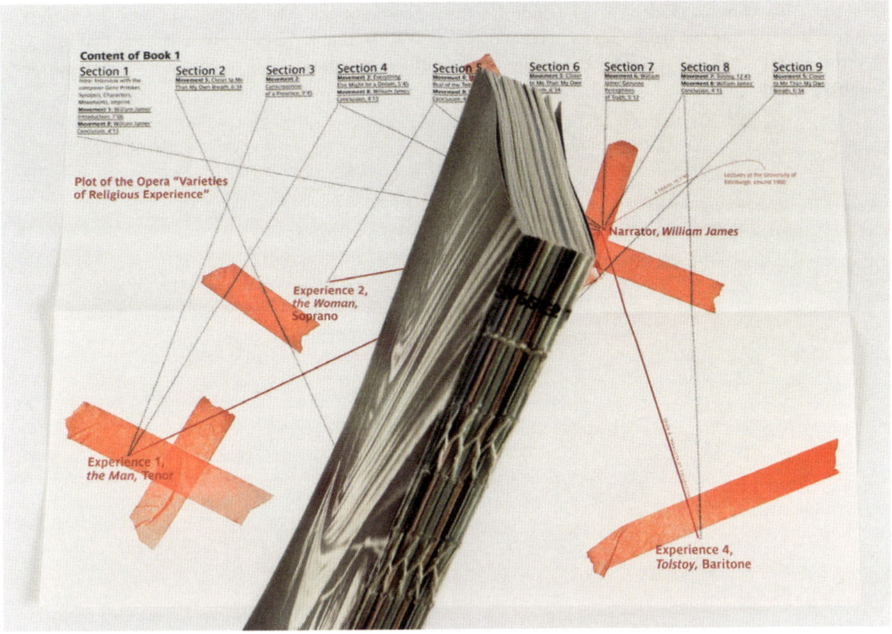
Content of Book 1
Section 1
Section 2
Section 3
Section 4
Section 6
Section 7
Section 8
Section 9
Plot of the Opera "Varieties of Religious Experience"
Narrator, William James
Experience 2, the Woman, Soprano
Experience 1, the Man, Tenor
Experience 4, Tolstoy, Baritone

The Opera "Varieties of Religious Experience"
Score

Score

Design: Alba Durana. **Title:** World Guide Gesture. **Description:** The project analyzes the variety of gestures that are internationally understood and seeks all those that have different meanings that may lead to error, thereby helping travelers from different countries. **School:** IDEP Institut Superior de Disseny. **Country:** Spain.

BÚSQUEDA
POR GESTOS
Un gesto con múltiples
significados.

HOLA
ALEGRIA
FELIZ
JAPÓN
Ásia

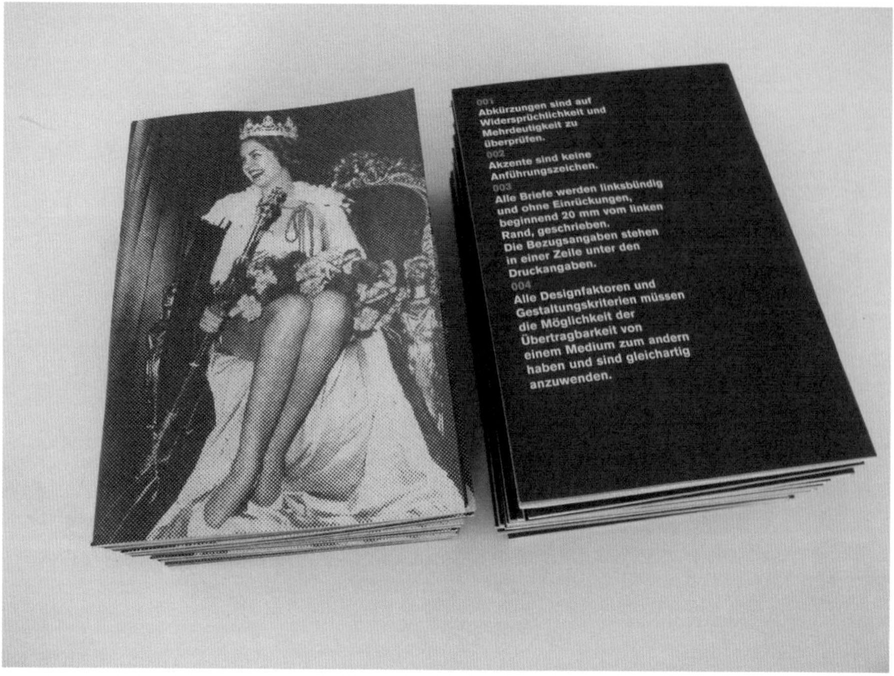

Design: Alexander Brade, Andreas Strack, Christoph Kronenberg, Florian Renschke, Linnea Erlich, Marijana Babic, Michaela Dechert, Oliver Schendzielorz, Patrick Gasselsdorfer, Pawel Napiorkowski, Rade Matic. **Title:** Bitte lasst die Blumen leben! (Please let the flowers live!). **Description:** What is good, what is bad and what is ugly within design? These questions were the starting point of a three-day workshop in the Faculty of Design, here in Darmstadt. We separated students into three groups (good, bad and ugly) with each one gathering representative statements, work samples, or visuals in the university library. The three groups then presented the collected materials to each other. This process immediately sparked a discussion as we found that categorising design works, designer statements and general design rules was extremely difficult, some even said it was wrong. Who were we to judge? And who were those designers who in turn judge others? We decided to display the collected statements and images in a single publication without any commentary. The result is an eclectic compilation that questions rules, doctrines and design education in general. And it's up to the reader to decide whether he or she believes a design is good, bad or ugly. In addition to these doctrines, we decided to show flowers of all kinds and from all kinds of sources as flowers are something almost everybody can relate to in a positive way. But if an image or a representation of a flower is good, bad or ugly is again up to the individual. **School:** University of Applied Sciences Darmstadt. **Country:** Germany.

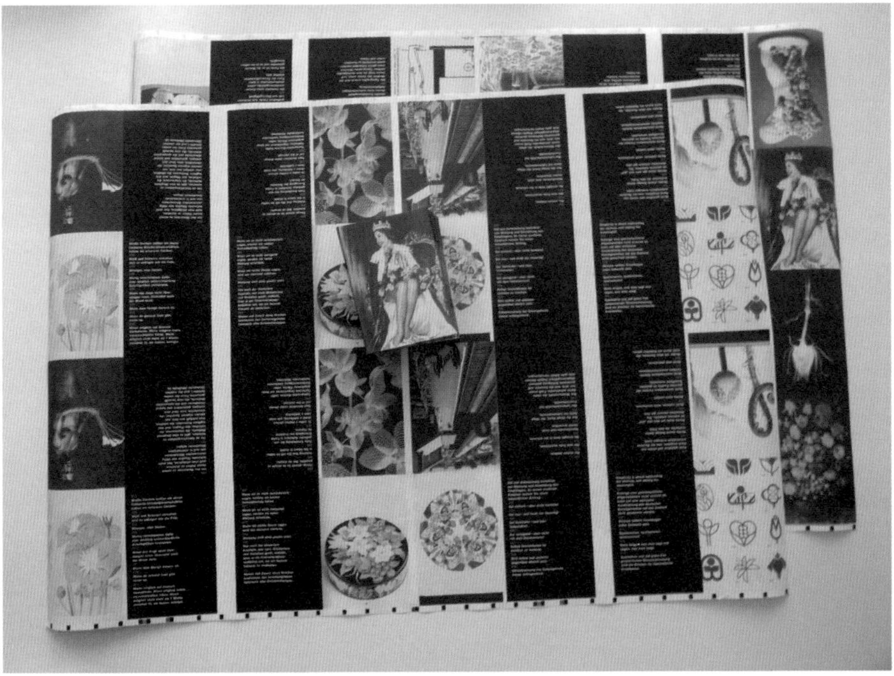

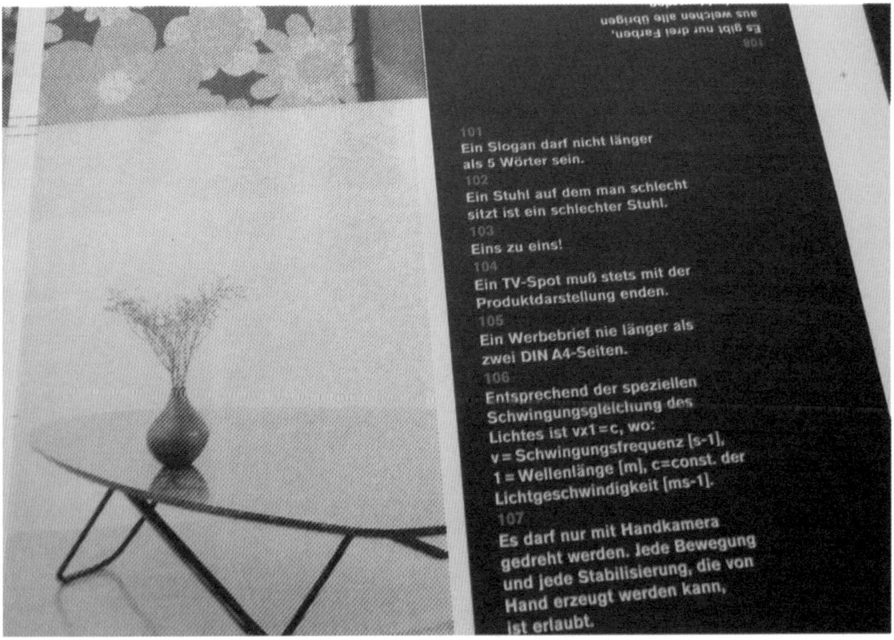
108
Es gibt nur drei Farben,
aus welchen alle übrigen
101
Ein Slogan darf nicht länger
als 5 Wörter sein.
102
Ein Stuhl auf dem man schlecht
sitzt ist ein schlechter Stuhl.
103
Eins zu eins!
104
Ein TV-Spot muß stets mit der
Produktdarstellung enden.
105
Ein Werbebrief nie länger als
zwei DIN A4-Seiten.
106
Entsprechend der speziellen
Schwingungsgleichung des
Lichtes ist vx1=c, wo:
v= Schwingungsfrequenz [s-1],
1= Wellenlänge [m], c=const. der
Lichtgeschwindigkeit [ms-1].
107
Es darf nur mit Handkamera
gedreht werden. Jede Bewegung
und jede Stabilisierung, die von
Hand erzeugt werden kann,
ist erlaubt.

A man is pumping water into the
cistern which supplies the drinking
water of a house.
BILDER VOM
KÜNSTLER

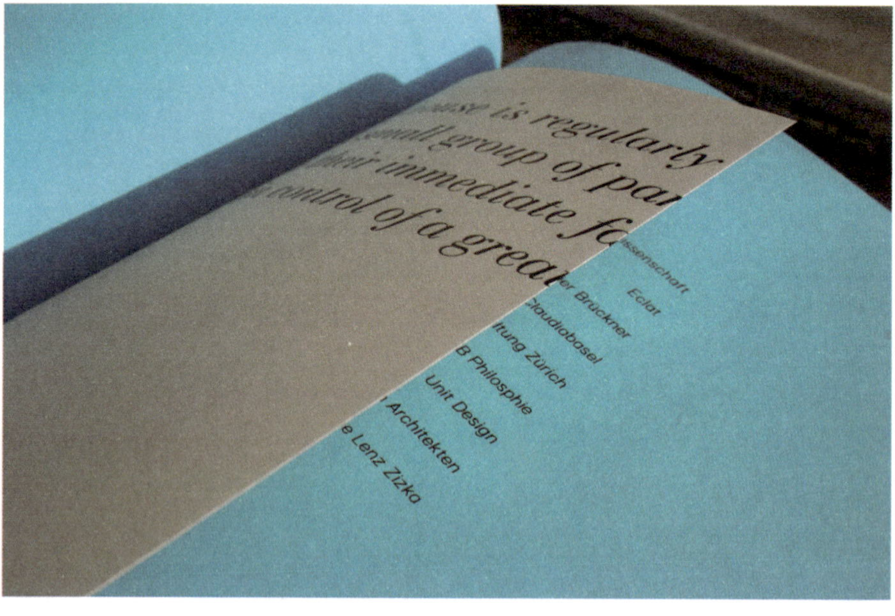
is regularly
small group of par
their immediate fo
control of a great
ssenschaft
Eclat
er Brückner
Claudiobasel
ltung Zürich
B Philosophie
Unit Design
Architekten
e Lenz Zizka

Design: Alexander Horn and Hwan Lee. **Title:** A man is pumping water… **Description:** This publication addresses the question: Is design a science? Sixteen interviews on 250 pages with renown German and Swiss designers on their approach to design and whether or not they think that design is an art or science or both. **School:** University of Applied Sciences Darmstadt. **Country:** Germany.

Design: Antonio García Cárceles. **Title:** 56f. **Description:** Experimental fanzine of design and culture. Printed in two colours on newspaper. It has an antique feel, which is achieved with typography, faded colours and sizes based on old, large-format fanzines that contrast with the modern and dynamic layout of today's fanzines. **School:** Escuela Superior de Diseño Región de Murcia. **Country:** Spain.

/INTRO
i Nº0 Diseño+Cultura año1
publicación gratuita mayo2010◊julio2010
Garamond Premier Pro Pantone 4584U
editor&director◊Jorge Arias diseñador◊Antonio García
redactor adjunto◊Micré Omar
marketing◊Josh Air redactor jefe◊Irene Martínez
relaciones públicas◊Elena Ortiz coordinador◊Max Libu
www.ifanzine.com asasdeicaro@gmail.com

Design: Bea Bascuñán Martínez. **Title:** Si nadie habla de las cosas que importan. **Description:** *'Si nadie habla de las cosas que importan'* (If Nobody Speaks of Remarkable Things, title from the book of Jon McGregor) is a personal point of view about graphic design in the different aspects of my life and about how I live it in my everyday life. It is also a project about my working process and a series of personal exercises that help me face the different projects I may have to solve. **School:** BAU, Escola Superior de Disseny. **Country:** Spain.

SI NADIE HABLA DE LAS COSAS QUE IMPORTAN*

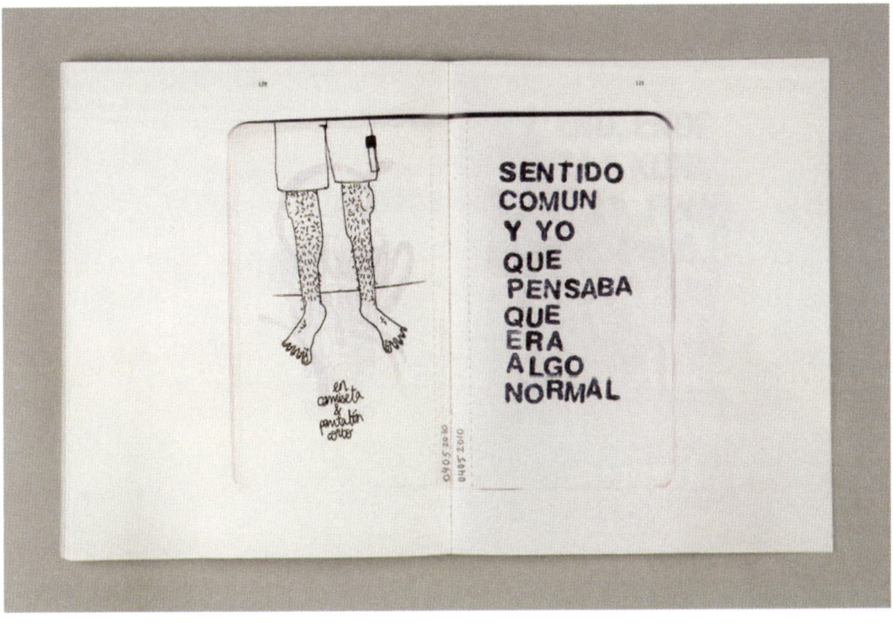
SENTIDO COMUN Y YO QUE PENSABA QUE ERA ALGO NORMAL
en camiseta & pantalón corto
0405 2010
0405 2010

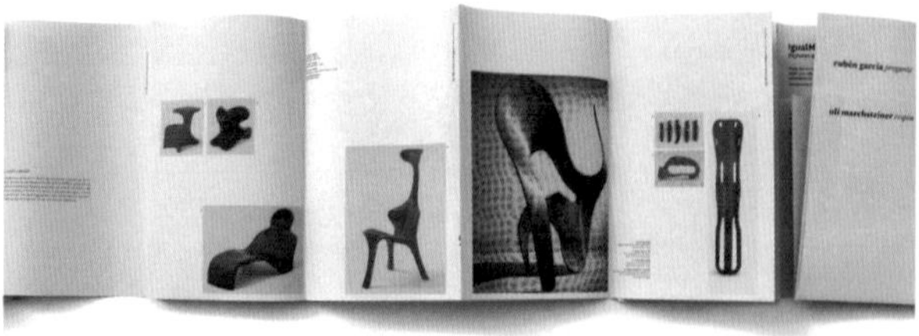
rubén garcía pregunta
uli marchsteiner respon

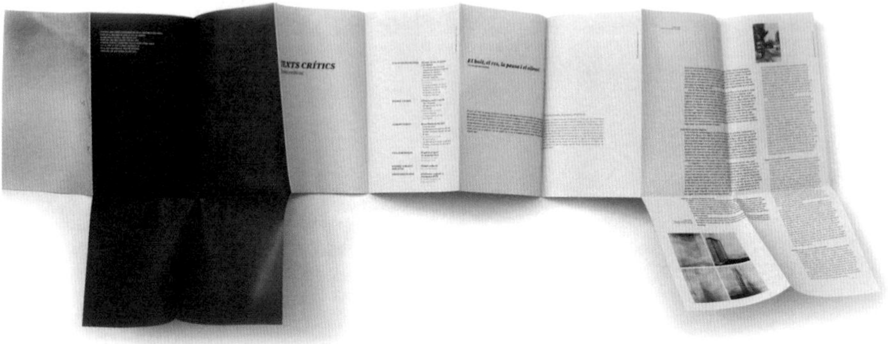
TEXTS CRÍTICS
El buit, el res, la pausa i el silenci

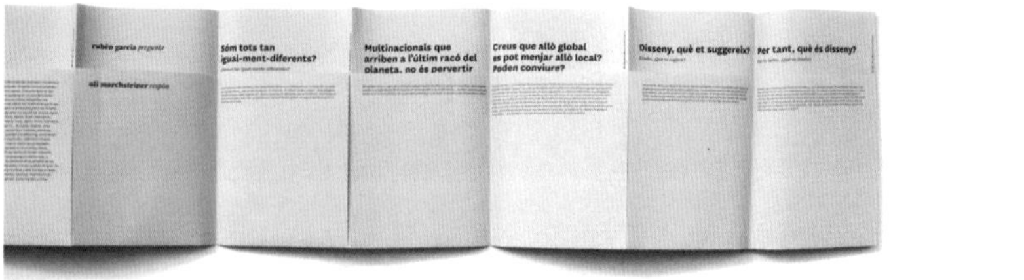
rubén garcía pregunta
uli marchsteiner respon
Sóm tots tan igual-ment-diferents?
Multinacionals que arriben a l'últim racó del Planeta, no és pervertir
Creus que allò global es pot menjar allò local? Poden conviure?
Disseny, què et suggereix?
Per tant, què és disseny?

entre
vista
a
uli
march-
steiner
IgualMentDiferents
rubén garcía pregunta
uli marchsteiner respon
Sóm tots tan igual-ment-diferents?

Design: Bet Puigbò Gassó. **Title:** Gap, nothing, break and silent. **Description:** Design of an experimental format for a publication that reflects on the importance of emptiness, nothingness, pause and silence. Articles, critical texts, images and interviews. Empty and full game. Collapsible and expandable. Up and down. You can do a traditional reading of the book or fully deploy until it becomes an object. The rhythms change, and each page breaks with the previous. **School:** ELISAVA Escola Superior de Disseny i Enginyeria de Barcelona. **Country:** Spain.

Design: Christoph Reichert. **Title:** Tyrannei des Augenblicks (vanitas vanitatum). **Description:** Our everyday life is stamped by continuously threatening deadlines and permanent lack of time. This book project visualises this modern lifestyle but also tries to show ways to decelerate. When you start flipping through the book, you are attracted to different images, text and colour. But you aren't able to get any information from it – just excitement. This feeling refers to sapping that can occur when watching your television programme and also shows that you cannot get any valuable information from it. At the moment you're separating the booklet into its five colours, you get the chance to look at one thing at a time. This moment of separation is my core element of deceleration. Those five smaller booklets you're getting in the end describe five factors of acceleration in modern society. **School:** University of Applied Sciences Darmstadt. **Country:** Germany.

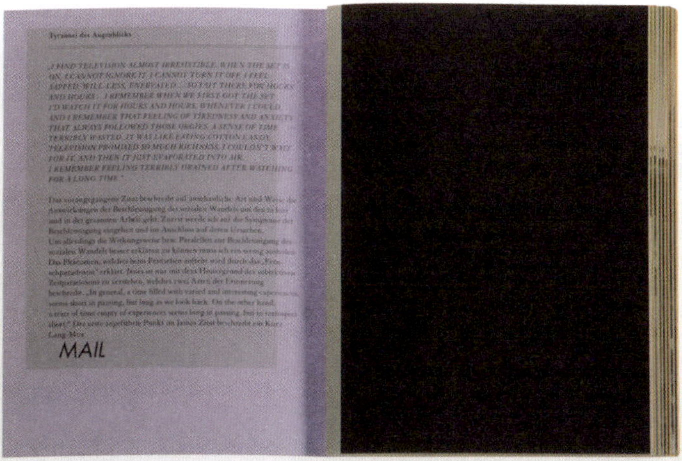
Tyrannei des Augenblicks
MAIL

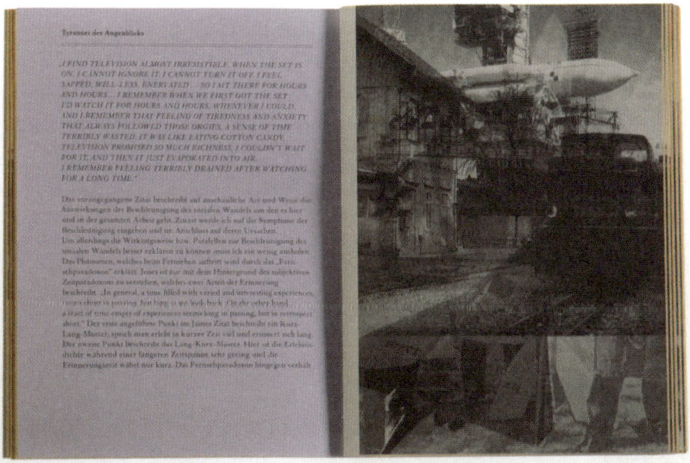
Tyrannei des Augenblicks

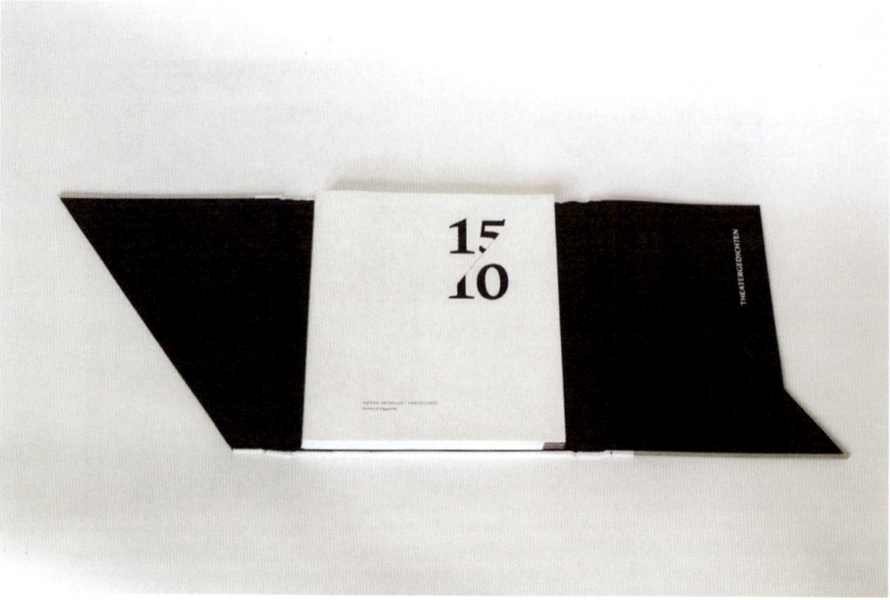
15
10
THEATERGEDICHTEN

Needcompany's
Sad face / Happy face
VERHALEN OVER MENSELIJKHEID
113
045

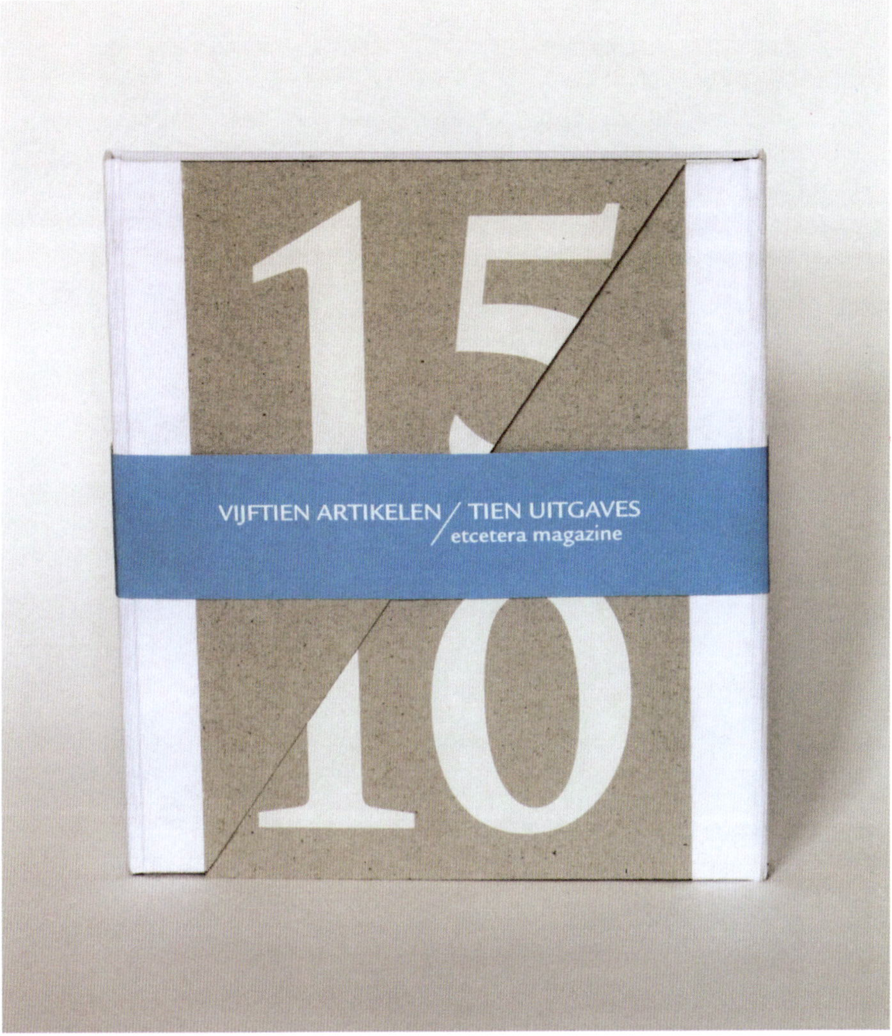

Design: Clinton Stringer. **Title:** 15 Articles | 11 Issues | Etcetera magazine. **Description:** This book is a collection of articles from the Belgian magazine for performing arts, 'Etcetera'. It comprises three sections: (1) a booklet of theatre poems found inside the front right cover; (2) the introduction consisting of the editorials from ten issues; and (3) the articles themselves – 15 interviews and essays chosen from the ten issues. **School:** Sint-Lukas Brussels University College of Art & Design. **Country:** Belgium.

Design: Edgar Ospina. **Title:** Mensajes No Enviados. **Description:** *'Mensajes No Enviados'* reflects on free speech, its vulnerability to risks and threats that continually undermine it. This project aims to raise awareness through images filled with metaphors and ironies to avoid the justification of the abuse of power by political dealing, business, religious institutions, misleading utopias and all kinds of repressive forces.

It consists of two books, the first is text and images illustrating examples of censorship in different latitudes as well as a posterior graphic project as a campaign of several lines of work. The cover is supported by a rubberband that plays both the chart and physically by censorsing the title. The second book is totally censored; it consists of replies but with all the texts converted into black blocks printed on vegetal paper, where the possibility of transparency is intermittently upset by the graphic blocks of ink. **School:** Istituto Europeo di Design IED, Madrid. **Country:** Spain.

Design: Elke Broothaers. **Title:** 'Maid' in China – The story behind your stuff . **Description:** In this book, I wanted to underscore how much we take our products – our stuff – for granted. Most of us buy and use products without ever thinking about their country of origin. That is why I thought it would be appropriate to highlight this aspect of so many daily utensils, devices and goods. I don't want this book to teach or preach, but primarily to help consumers be more aware of the origins of so many objects that have become key to our daily lives. The goal of this book is to inform readers about the journey these goods make, before they eventually are displayed in our shops and stores. Another goal of this book is to make bargain hunters aware of the background of these incredibly low-priced goods because glamorous goods aren't made in glamorous factories. **School:** Sint-Lukas Brussels University College of Art and Design. **Country:** Belgium.

05
In Chinese the word for 'crisis' is the same as the word for 'opportunity'?
MADE IN CHINA

02
China adapted the ideas of Lenin who had successfully achieved a revolution in Russia in 1917

Recycled Masterpieces
Cristiana Couceiro
52
53
speak.
Opernhaus Zürich
"I am a freelance illustrator, working and living in Lisbon, Portugal.
I have been making collages since I was a kid. I used to sit on the floor and tear up magazines for hours, joining pieces of paper of different shapes and colours together. Later I learned how to use a pair of scissors and some glue and started filling notebooks, walls and furniture. Then I just learned how to edit pictures on the computer and stopped gluing everywhere.
I collect memories, personal and collective, national and international. My collages are made from an assemblage of different forms, thus creating a new one. They may include newspaper titles, vintage photos, pieces of paper, portions of other artworks, book pages, placed on a new piece of paper."
Cristiana Couceiro

Geigy
Kik hält Insekten fern
Desogen
Geigy

Design: Ellen Van Huffel. **Title:** Cover. **Description:** 'Cover' is a book about Akzidenz Grotesk, its history, origin, uses and users who were the masters of 20th century design, their family and friends. It is a nearly a 200-page love letter to a typeface, divided into five color-coded chapters. It's a wide and personal selection of beautiful things made with Akzidenz Grotesk. The cover does not have a traditional cover, but is neatly wrapped in a foldout, two-colour silkscreen-printed poster. **School:** Sint-Lukas Brussels University College of Art and Design. **Country:** Belgium.

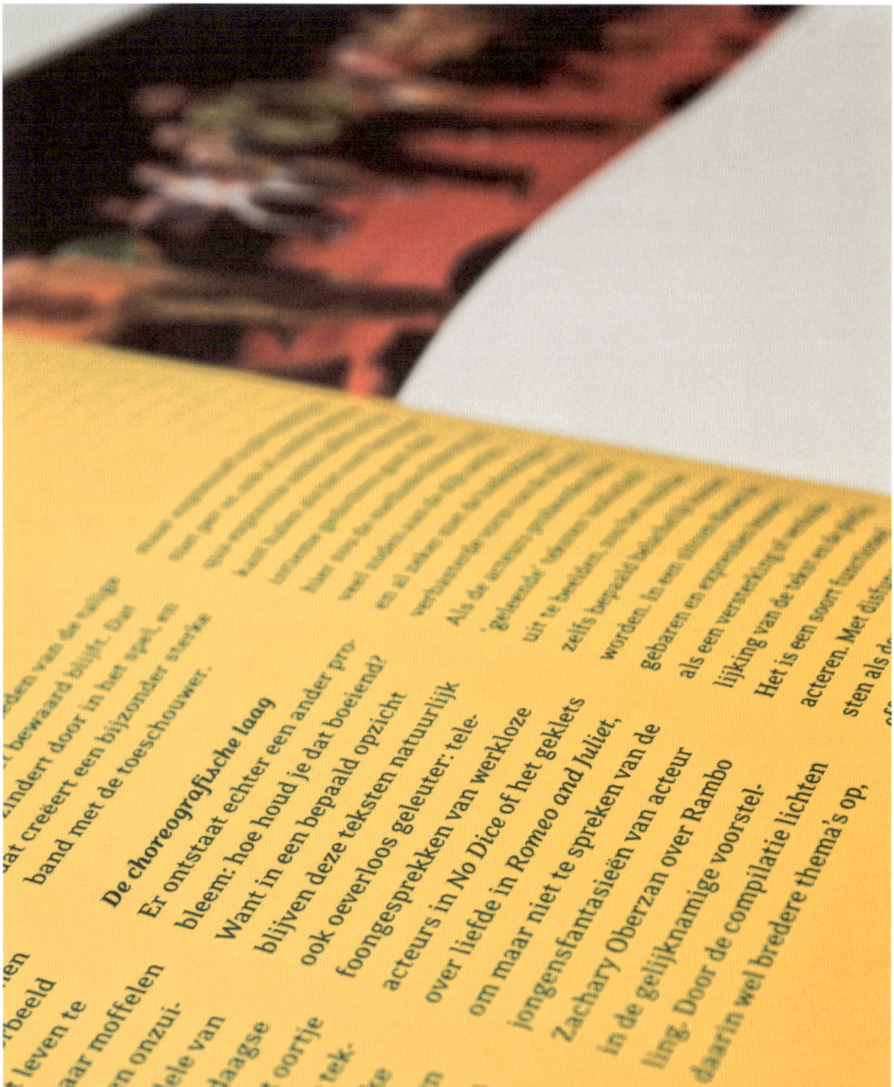
band met de toeschouwer.
De choreografische laag
Er ontstaat echter een ander pro-
bleem: hoe houd je dat boeiend?
Want in een bepaald opzicht
blijven deze teksten natuurlijk
ook oeverloos geleuter: tele-
foongesprekken van werkloze
acteurs in No Dice of het geklets
over liefde in Romeo and Juliet,
om maar niet te spreken van de
jongensfantasieën van acteur
Zachary Oberzan over Rambo
in de gelijknamige voorstel-
ling. Door de compilatie lichten
daarin wel bredere thema's op,

Design: Inge Van Ginderachter. **Title:** 10 x Etcetera. **Description:** This book is a collection of articles from the Belgian magazine for performing arts, *Etcetera*. **School:** Sint-Lukas Brussels University College of Art and Design. **Country:** Belgium.

Design: Laura Wells. **Title:** Brothers Grimm. **Description:** The brief was to create an illustrated book based on one of the children's stories by the Brothers Grimm. The approach was to use laser-cut illustrations from the pages to create the scenes in addition to incorporating handcrafted and typeset typography. The front cover was created using a hand-drawn illustration that has been engraved into leatherette. The title of the book has also been engraved for a subtle effect. A set of footprints are cut out from the cover, which was created using red cardstock to convey Little Red Riding Hood's footsteps. For the pages devoted to Little Red Riding Hood in the forest, the cutout illustrations work alongside flat artwork that has been created by stenciling with acrylic paint. For the detail of the forest cutout, the page opens out to a full forest scene. All cutout illustrations were hand cut and then laser cut for cleaner lines. **School:** Nottingham Trent University. **Country:** United Kingdom.

Little Red-Cap

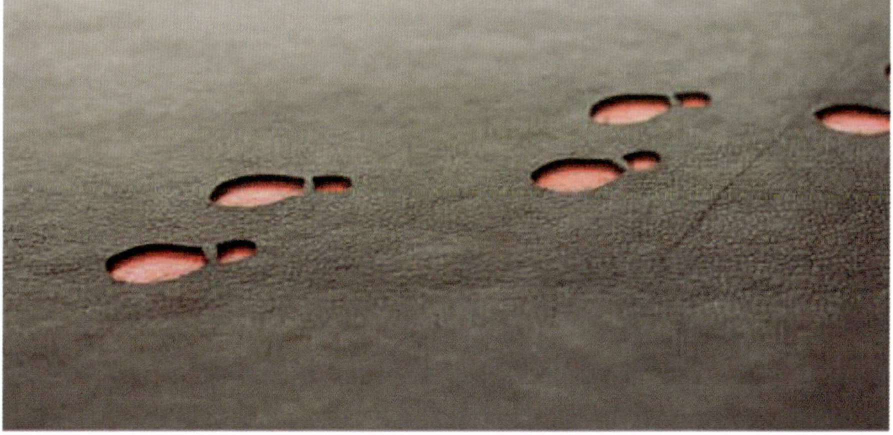

Design: Lorena Cardona Pérez. **Title:** ¡Menudo cambio! **Description:** *'¡Menudo cambio!'* is a children's educational book about climate change. This book uses graphic representation of information to explain simply and schematically what is happening on our planet. **School:** Escuela de Arte y Superior de Diseño de Valencia. **Country:** Spain.

Aguas residuales
Extracción
Pesca
Agricultura
El uso doméstico

(CUIDALA)

Design: Lucía Castro Triay. **Title:** Panoptic Magazine. **Description:** 'Panoptic Magazine' is a monographic magazine of leisure and identity that functions as social observations. The author's philosophy is based on transmitting contents clearly and directly, incorporating the idea of an anthropological perspective. Issue #1 is titled 'Outside Leisure'. **School:** ELISAVA Escola Superior de Disseny i Enginyeria de Barcelona. **Country:** Spain.

I AM
(ME RETRATO)

I AM

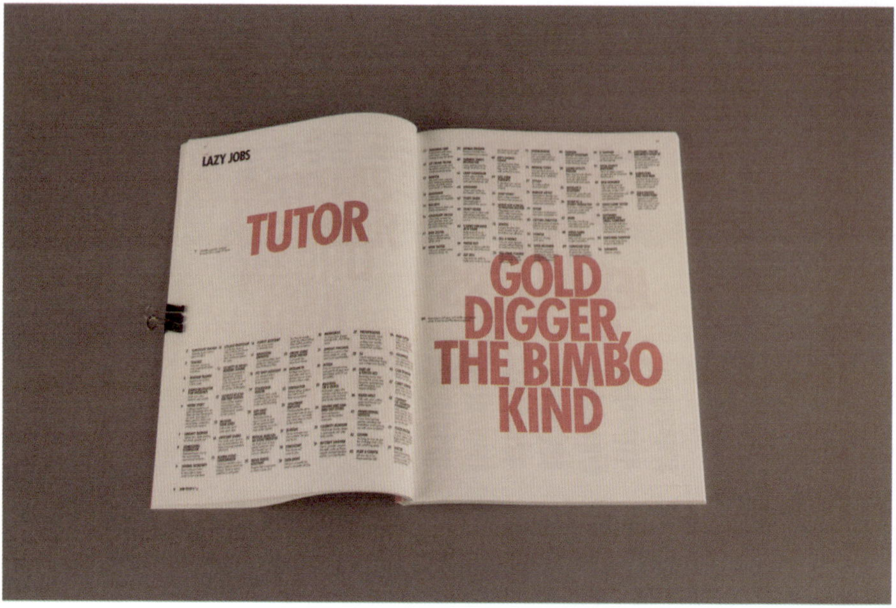
LAZY JOBS
TUTOR
GOLD DIGGER, THE BIMBO KIND

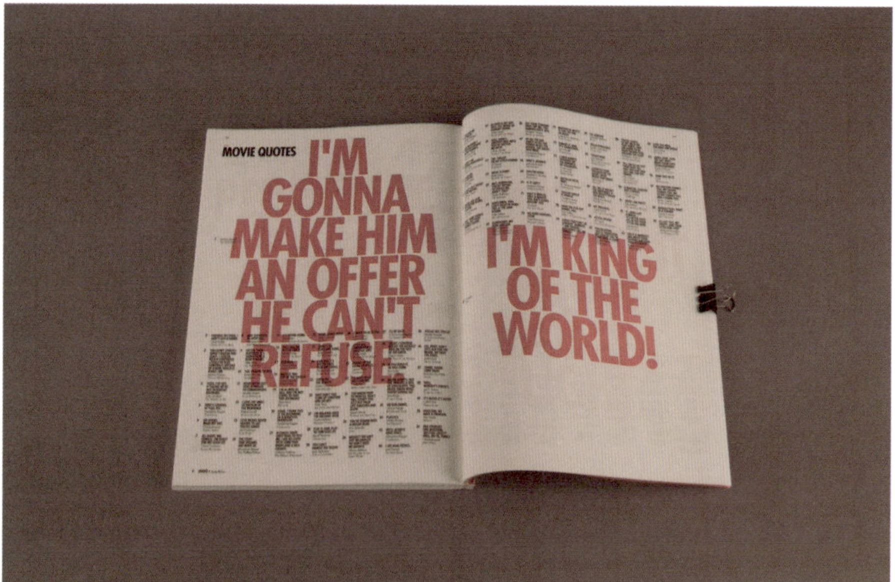
MOVIE QUOTES
I'M GONNA MAKE HIM AN OFFER HE CAN'T REFUSE.
I'M KING OF THE WORLD!

Design: Marc Monguilod Triola. **Title:** One Hundred One Hundreds. **Description:** A book that reflects on the absurd need of society to classify and order things. Using repetition as a theme, the book shows one hundred Top 100 lists, distributed in 100 double pages, showing the extent to which almost everything can be reduced to irrelevant lists such as the top 100 dog names. On the left page the position of number 1 is shown whereas the position of number 100 is shown on the right page. **School:** IDEP Institut Superior de Disseny. **Country:** Spain.

Design: Marc Monguilod Triola. **Title:** Trapped. **Description:** 'Trapped' represents all the people who have been repressed by a country or regime because they have raised their voices through culture. Created as eight pieces, this object-book literally hides different materials that have been censored or banned. This wasn't conceived as a book of information, but rather as a book to experience. **School:** IDEP Institut Superior de Disseny. **Country:** Spain.

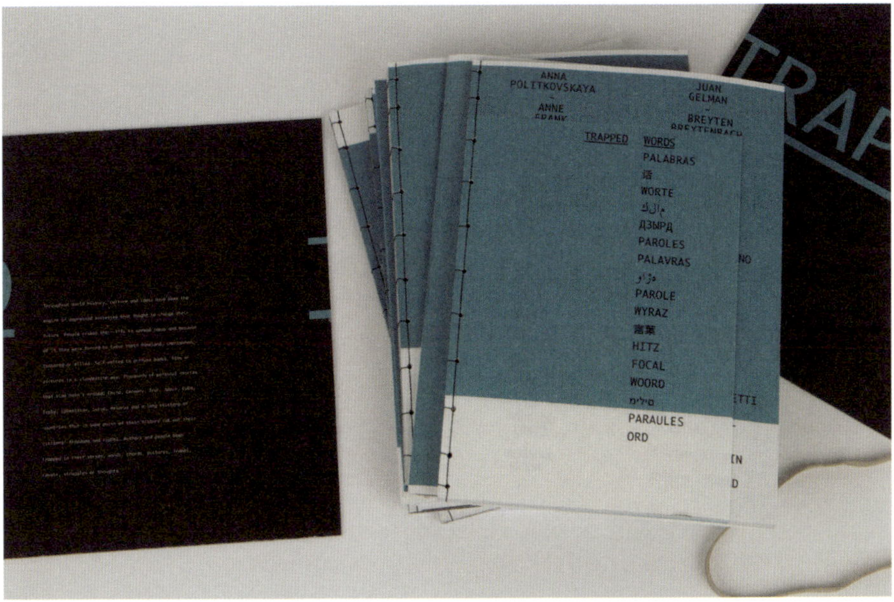
ANNA
POLITKOVSKAYA
ANNE
JUAN
GELMAN
BREYTEN
TRAPPED
WORDS
PALABRAS
话
WORTE
PAROLES
PALAVRAS
PAROLE
WYRAZ
HITZ
FOCAL
WOORD
מילים
PARAULES
ORD
TRAP

KAREEM AMER

THE MANKIND MANIFESTO
Building a world where we can live in
03
WASTE LESS
4 1/2 POUNDS
OF GARBAGE
A DAY

Design: Maria Ballestar. **Title:** The Mankind Manifesto. **Description:** The economic system that we are currently experiencing is based on consumption as a way of life and a source of satisfaction. We are now seeing the effects of the excesses of this system. A change is needed to move us out of this recession and toward a sustainable world development that will ensure that current needs are met, but one that at the same time allows for future development. The project consists of a public-oriented campaign to spread the idea of change through a sustainable development manifesto. The aim of this campaign is to encourage all individuals to change their habits. The challenge facing the design was to communicate these ideals in a sustainable way. The manifesto covers topics ranging from electricity consumption to the qualities of the politicians that we elect to the call for peace and nuclear disarmament. The primary tool to communicate these ideals is a book, even though its contents are also on the website. Two poster campaigns introduce and reinforce the subject, and a leaflet provides condensed information about the ideals of the manifesto, which encourages its readers in taking an active role in disseminating the manifesto's contents. **School:** Eina, Escola de Disseny i Art. **Country:** Spain.

Design: Matt Adams. **Title:** Visualising sound. **Description:** This book is based on the BBC Radio 4 show, 'The Unbelievable Truth'. A 120-page, perfect bound book documents six different methods of visualising sound in a literal sense. Each section is designated a colour taken from television test screens, and each page contains the relevant information in which the sound was documented. **School:** Nottingham Trent University. **Country:** United Kingdom.

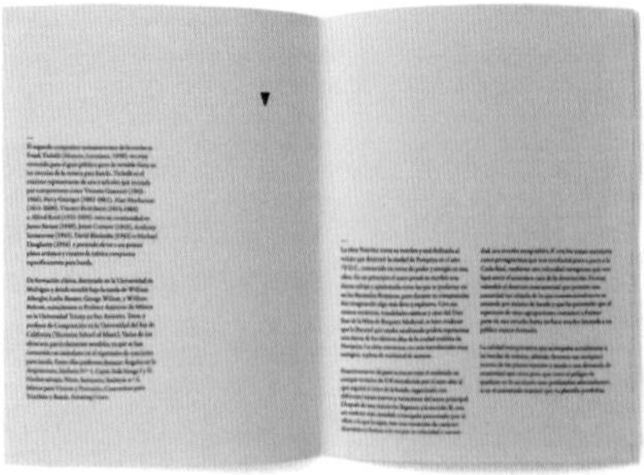

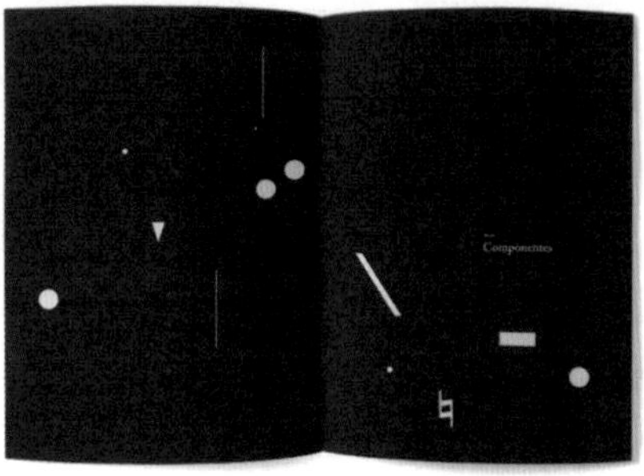

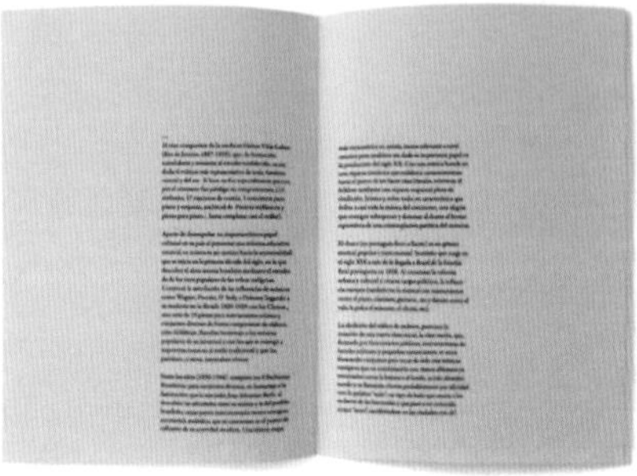

Design: Nahuel Marín Luriaud. **Title:** Extraordinary Concert. **Description:** Poster and programme of 'Extraordinary Concert' performed by the Conservatory Manuel Massotti Littel in the Auditorio Victor Villegas de Murcia. The graphic design was created from the decomposition of the musical symbols. As for the layout of the programme, the texts were placed at different heights, as if we wrote notes on a pentagram. **School:** Escuela Superior de Diseño Región de Murcia. **Country:** Spain.

Concierto
Extraordinario
9 Feb 20:30 h.
Conservatorio
Superior de Música
de Murcia
Manuel Massotti Littel
Auditorio Víctor Villegas
Región de Murcia
Entrada—10€
Puntos de venta—Auditorio Víctor Villegas
www.auditoriomurcia.org
Banda del
Conservatorio Superior
Director de la Banda: Ángel Quereda Barceló
'Candide Oberture' —Leonard Bernstein (Arr. Walter Beeler)—
'Vesuvius' —Frank Ticheli—
Orquesta Sinfónica del
Conservatorio Superior
Director de la Orquesta Sinfónica: José Miguel Rodilla
'West Side Story (Symphonic Dances)' —Leonard Bernstein—
Orquesta Sinfónica y Coro del
Conservatorio Superior
Director del Coro: Ángel Martín Matute
Director de la Orquesta: José Miguel Rodilla
'Chichester Psalms' —Leonard Bernstein—
'Choros n.10, Rasga o Coração' —Heitor Villa-Lobos—

DAS BUNTE BUCH
VERHALTENSGESTÖRTER TIERE
von Patrick Bonato

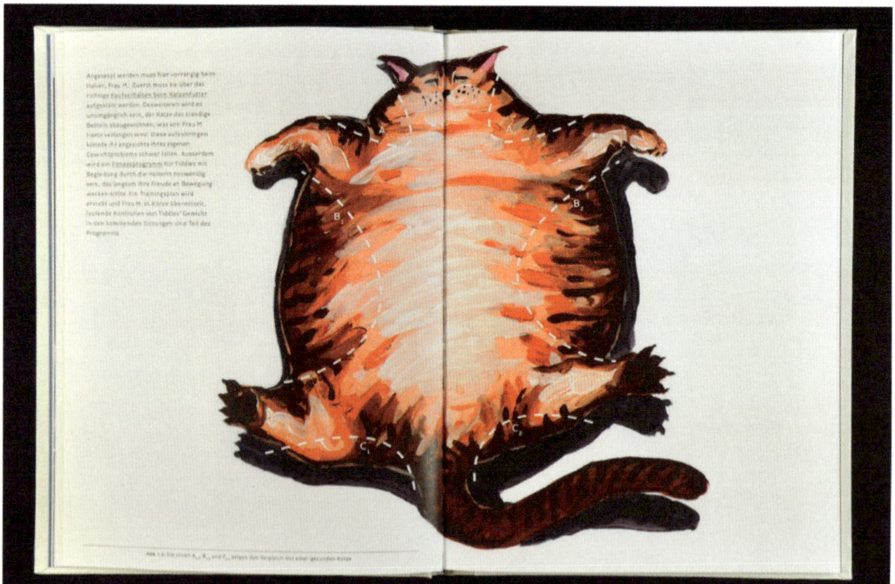

Design: Patrick Bonato. **Title:** Das Bunte Buch verhaltensgestörter Tiere. **Description:** There are about 2,070,000 cats, 720,000 dogs, 220,000 cage birds, 580,000 rodents and bunnies as well as 4.06 million tank and pond fish in Austria, and almost as many pet owners. Nevertheless, only 17 animal psychologists are offering their services in the country. Nobody knows how many pets and pet owners could use their help. For a book on abnormal animal behaviour called *'Das bunte Buch verhaltensgestörter Tiere'*, six animal psychologists from Austria and Switzerland agreed to be interviewed about their work. In this diploma thesis, the five most interesting patient histories are described and illustrated. **School:** University of Applied Arts Vienna. **Country:** Austria.

Design: Philippe Fernandez. **Title:** Moustache. **Description:** *'Moustache'* is a bilingual catalogue of a fictitious convention of moustached men in Barcelona. **School:** ELISAVA Escola Superior de Disseny i Enginyeria de Barcelona. **Country:** Spain.

Tipos
de bigote
Types
of moustache

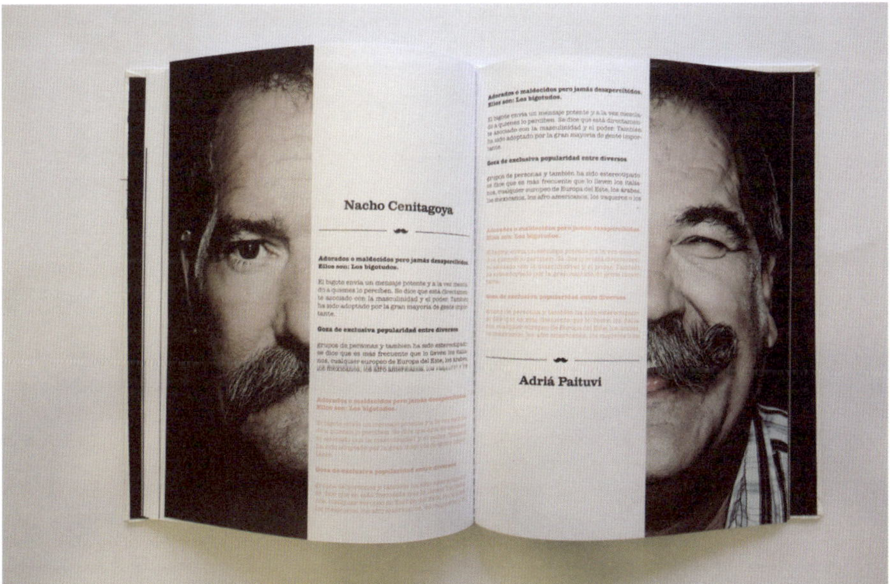
Nacho Cenitagoya
Adriá Paituvi

Design: Raquel López. **Title:** This is the only place where death succor life. **Description:** This book makes tribute to the engravings of William Cowper, the works of anatomist Bidloo Govard and plagiarism in the 17th century. It is inspired by the book that the Institute of History of Medicine and Science would give its members to disseminate, promote and recognize the work of documentation, research, information, protection and conservation undertaken by the Institute since its founding by Jose Maria López Piñero. Structured in three parts with three leaflets, this book offers introduction help readers understand the Institute, its goals, projects and publications. In the second part with texts, J.M. López Piñero narrates the evolution of anatomic illustration from the 15th to 19th centuries. And the third part shows the reproduction and restoration of Cowper prints. **School:** Escuela de Arte y Superior de Diseño de Valencia. **Country:** Spain.

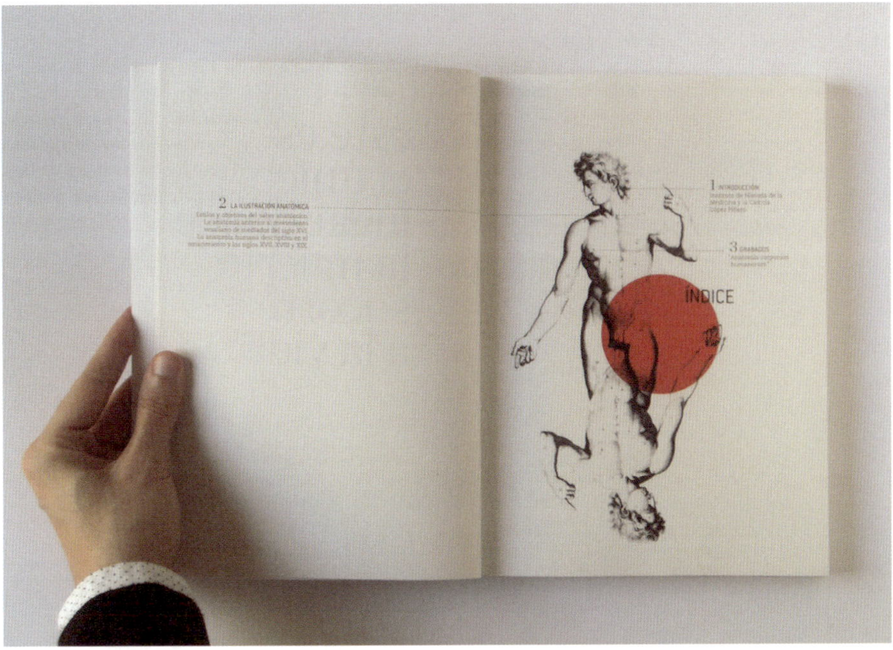
2 LA ILUSTRACIÓN ANATÓMICA
ÍNDICE

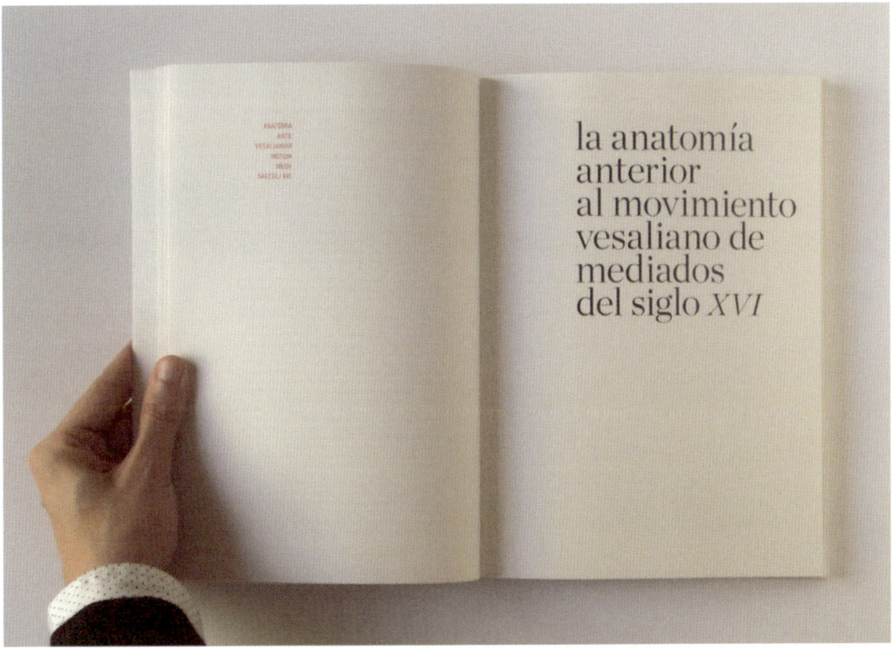
ANATOMIA
ANTE
VESALIANUM
MOTUM
MEDII
SAECULI XVI
la anatomía
anterior
al movimiento
vesaliano de
mediados
del siglo *XVI*

Design: Saara Järvinen. **Title:** Devoted to dirt. **Description:** In self-sufficient households, people used to have devoted, long-lasting relationships with objects. Unlike today, waste equalled failure. Cleaning is a creative way of making sense of our physical surroundings and forging bonds with the things we own. If the processes of getting dirty and clean are made equal through the use of objects, we can regain control of ownership. By creating associations between certain objects and natural creatures that have their characteristic behaviourz and expectations, I can blur the experience of dirt. The decay of these objects becomes acceptable, and cleaning them becomes natural. Cleaning tasks are repeated day after day, generation after generation. I want to show that a delicate caring relationship between the owner and the object is hidden in this routine. **School:** Design Academy Eindhoven. **Country:** The Netherlands.

CLEANING
ENCYCLOPEDIA
42 WINDOWS
WINDOWS 43
16 FLOORS
Floors of all materials can be cleaned by vacuuming, mopping and wiping
CARPETS 17
Carpets should be vacuumed with a floor brush

Design: Sebastian Thönnes. **Title:** Sein scheinen. **Description:** A homage to the beauty of mistakes and especially to those orphans and widows in typography. The entire book consists of poems that were made and written from the typographic orphans and widows found in the classic novel department within the Darmstadt city library. **School:** University of Applied Sciences Darmstadt. **Country:** Germany.

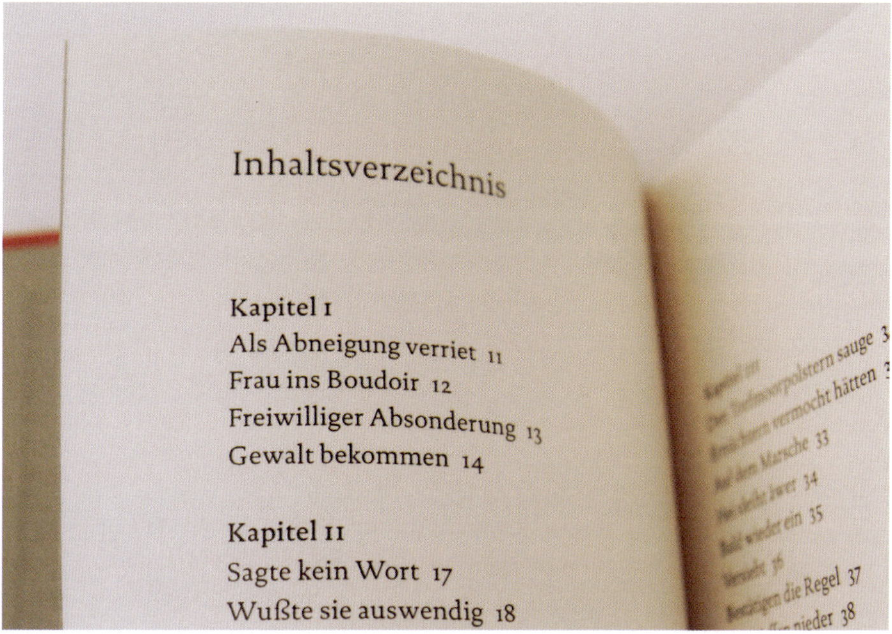

Inhaltsverzeichnis

Kapitel I
Als Abneigung verriet 11
Frau ins Boudoir 12
Freiwilliger Absonderung 13
Gewalt bekommen 14

Kapitel II
Sagte kein Wort 17
Wußte sie auswendig 18

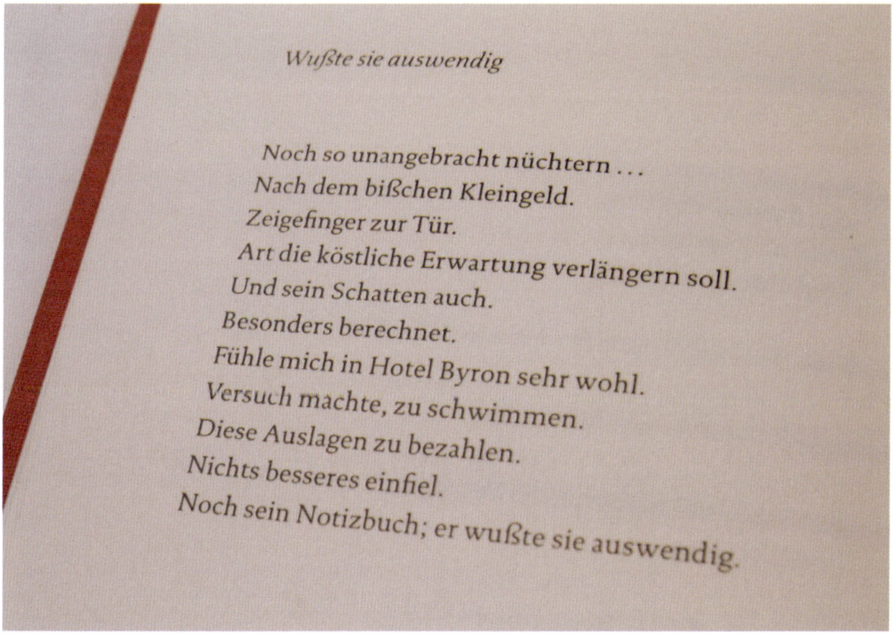

Wußte sie auswendig

Noch so unangebracht nüchtern . . .
Nach dem bißchen Kleingeld.
Zeigefinger zur Tür.
Art die köstliche Erwartung verlängern soll.
Und sein Schatten auch.
Besonders berechnet.
Fühle mich in Hotel Byron sehr wohl.
Versuch machte, zu schwimmen.
Diese Auslagen zu bezahlen.
Nichts besseres einfiel.
Noch sein Notizbuch; er wußte sie auswendig.

Exhibitions

Design: Alexander Brade, Alice Mattheß, Andreas Knapp, Anja Grunert, Anna Kraus, Charlotte Gunia, Christina Löber, Denis Kreuzer, Elisa Scheichl, Friedl Lesch, Julia Krust, Katharina Göbel, Kristina Voll, Linnea Erlich, Lukas Fiala, Marijana Babic, Paul Raabe, Rade Matic, Raphael Schifferdecker, Sina Schindler, Tina Michi, Vital Kurz. **Title:** Show Down (Exhibition). **Description:** One-day exhibition at the University of Applied Sciences Darmstadt, Faculty of Design with performances, films, installations, videos and graphic work on the subject of conflict. **School:** University of Applied Sciences Darmstadt. **Country:** Germany.

Design: Miriam Thijssen. **Title:** All You Need Is Oil. **Description:** 'All You Need Is Oil' uses a love story as an allegory for the role that oil plays in our society. The duration of the love affair, 1945 (the end of WWII) through 2030 (the beginning of WWIII), reflects the height of our world's oil production. **School:** Willem de Kooning Academy. **Country:** The Netherlands.

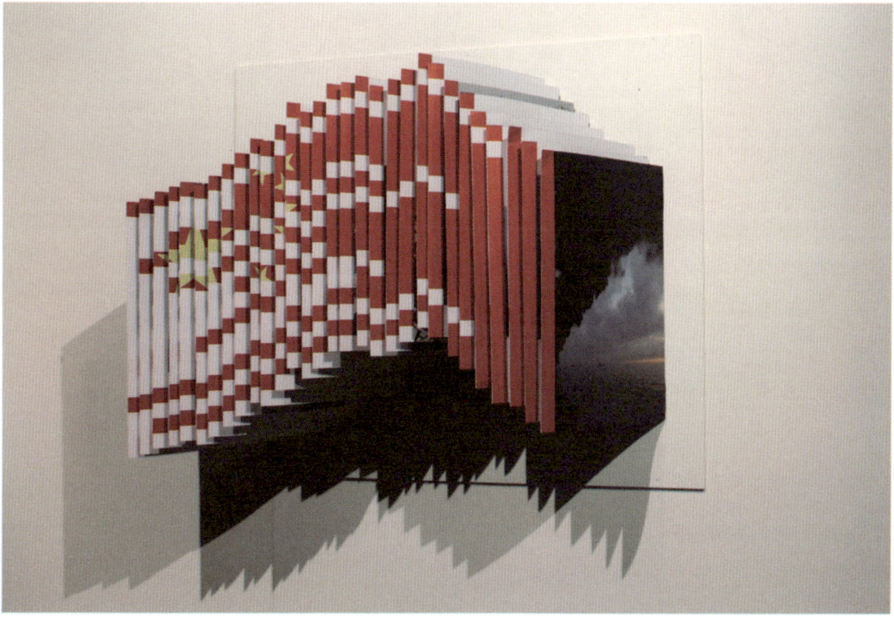

I just can't get
through you.

Illustration

Design: Andre Meca. **Title:** Sustainability. **Description:** Based on scientific and technological research, this collage illustration was made in fuction to deal with many of today's important topics: climate change, pollution, environment, communication and green transportation. Where research contributes to understand these topics, finds alternatives, proposes new solutions: research can improve the world and the society we live in. Sustainability can be the answer, it has to move us, we need to do something about ourselves and the world we all live in. **School:** Escola Superior de Artes e Design de Caldas da Rainha. **Country:** Portugal.

SUSTAINABILITY

Design: Anne Manteleers. **Title:** Knight Pietro. **Description:** 'Knight Pietro' is an imaginairy person who is looking for the perfect house in Brussels. He doesn't look in obvious places but travels along famous buildings where he has conversations with people who tell him stories about the history of the place. This is a series of 10 illustrations which guide the reader trough the city and show 'Knight Pietro' in his search for the place he wants to stay. **School:** Sint-Lukas Brussels University College of Art & Design. **Country:** Belgium.

HET CENTRUM VAN BRUSSEL IS OPGEDEELD IN EEN HOOG GEBIED EN EEN LAAG GEBIED. DE OVERGANG TUSSEN DEZE DELEN SITUEERT ZICH ROND HET GERECHTSPLEIN. HET LAGE GEBIED STREKT ZICH GROFWEG UIT ROND DE GROTE MARKT. RIDDER PIETRO BEZOEKT HIER VOORAL DAT LAGE GEBIED.
N°2
RIDDER PIETRO BEZOEKT HET GEBIED ROND DE GROTE MARKT
MOEILIJK VINDBAAR LIJKT ME WEL WAT. HIER ZOU IK WEL WILLEN WONEN.
DIT IS DE OUDSTE KERK VAN BRUSSEL, MAAR OOK DE MOEILIJKST VINDBARE.
eglise st. Nicolas (BOTERSTRAAT)
BINNEN HANGT ER EEN KLEIN SCHILDERIJ VAN MIJ.
de koninklijke muntschouwburg (MUNTPLEIN)
THEATRE ROYALE DE LA MONNAIE
DE NAAM VAN DEZE SCHOUWBURG KOMT VAN EEN MUNTSLAGERIJ DIE HIER VOORDIEN WAS GEVESTIGD
IN 1830 IS HET DOOR EEN BRAND VERWOEST. IK HEB DE WEDEROPBOUW GELEID.
sint Michiels en sint Goedele kathedraal. (SINTER-GOEDELEVOORPLEIN)
DEZE KERK HEET OFFICIEEL "SINT MICHIELS-KATHEDRAAL".
IN DE VOLKSMOND OOK DE "SINTE GOEDELEKERK", MAAR OFFICIEEL WORDT HIJ NIET VERNOEMD OMDAT HET VATICAAN MIJ NIET ERKENT ALS HEILIGE.
DIT GEBOUW IS HET KROONJUWEEL VAN JULES ANSPACH.
IK BEN EEN VAN DE BEELDHOUWERS.
de Beurs (BEURSPLEIN)
onze-lieve-vrouw van de finistère kerk (NIEUWSTRAAT)
IK WORD SOMS OOK DE OUDSTE BURGER VAN BRUSSEL GENOEMD.
BINNEN IN DE KERK STAAT ER EEN BEELD VAN MIJ.
manneken pis (EIKSTRAAT)
DIT MANNEKE IS NET ZOALS IK TOT RIDDER GESLAGEN. HIJ IS OOK TOT DE ADEL VERHEVEN EN IS ONDER ANDERE EREBURGER EN EREBRIGADIER.
RP
IN DIT AVONTUUR BEZOEKT RIDDER PIETRO EEN AANTAL GEBOUWEN ROND DE GROTE MARKT. HIJ SPREEKT ER TELKENS MET EEN AANTAL PERSONEN DIE IETS TE MAKEN HEBBEN MET HET GEBOUW IN KWESTIE.

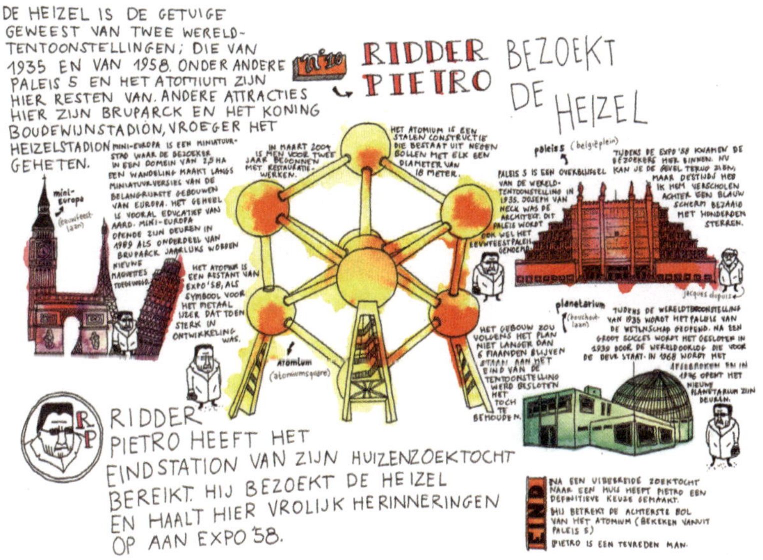
DE HEIZEL IS DE GETUIGE GEWEEST VAN TWEE WERELDTENTOONSTELLINGEN; DIE VAN 1935 EN VAN 1958. ONDER ANDERE PALEIS 5 EN HET ATOMIUM ZIJN HIER RESTEN VAN. ANDERE ATTRACTIES HIER ZIJN BRUPARCK EN HET KONING BOUDEWIJNSTADION, VROEGER HET HEIZELSTADION GEHETEN.
N°10
RIDDER PIETRO BEZOEKT DE HEIZEL
MINI-EUROPA IS EEN MINIATUURSTAD WAAR DE BEZOEKER IN EEN DOMEIN VAN 2,5 HA EEN WANDELING MAAKT LANGS MINIATUURVERSIES VAN DE BELANGRIJKSTE GEBOUWEN VAN EUROPA. HET GEHEEL IS VOORAL EDUCATIEF VAN AARD. MINI-EUROPA OPENDE ZIJN DEUREN IN 1989 ALS ONDERDEEL VAN BRUPARCK. JAARLIJKS WORDEN NIEUWE MAQUETTES TOEGEVOEGD.
mini-Europa (eeuwfeestlaan)
IN MAART 2004 IS MEN VOOR TWEE JAAR BEGONNEN MET RESTAURATIEWERKEN.
HET ATOMIUM IS EEN STALEN CONSTRUCTIE DIE BESTAAT UIT NEGEN BOLLEN MET ELK EEN DIAMETER VAN 18 METER.
HET ATOMIUM IS EEN RESTANT VAN EXPO '58, ALS SYMBOOL VOOR HET METAAL IJZER DAT TOEN STERK IN ONTWIKKELING WAS.
Atomium (atomiumsquare)
HET GEBOUW ZOU VOLGENS HET PLAN NIET LANGER DAN 6 MAANDEN BLIJVEN STAAN. AAN HET EIND VAN DE TENTOONSTELLING WERD BESLOTEN HET TOCH TE BEHOUDEN.
paleis 5 (belgiëplein)
PALEIS 5 IS EEN OVERBLIJFSEL VAN DE WERELDTENTOONSTELLING IN 1935. JOSEPH VAN NECK WAS DE ARCHITECT. DIT PALEIS WORDT OOK WEL HET EEUWFEESTPALEIS GENOEMD.
TIJDENS DE EXPO '58 KWAMEN DE BEZOEKERS HIER BINNEN. NU KAN JE DE GEVEL TERUG ZIEN, MAAR DESTIJDS HEB IK HEM VERSCHOLEN ACHTER EEN BLAUW SCHERM BEZAAID MET HONDERDEN STERREN.
jacques dupuis
planetarium (bouchoutlaan)
TIJDENS DE WERELDTENTOONSTELLING VAN 1935 WORDT HET PALEIS VAN DE WETENSCHAP GEOPEND. NA EEN GROOT SUCCES WORDT HET GESLOTEN IN 1939 DOOR DE WERELDOORLOG DIE VOOR DE DEUR STAAT. IN 1968 WORDT HET AFGEBROKEN EN IN 1976 OPENT HET NIEUWE PLANETARIUM ZIJN DEUREN.
RP
RIDDER PIETRO HEEFT HET EINDSTATION VAN ZIJN HUIZENZOEKTOCHT BEREIKT. HIJ BEZOEKT DE HEIZEL EN HAALT HIER VROLIJK HERINNERINGEN OP AAN EXPO '58.
EIND
NA EEN UITGEBREIDE ZOEKTOCHT NAAR EEN HUIS HEEFT PIETRO EEN DEFINITIEVE KEUZE GEMAAKT.
HIJ BETREKT DE ACHTERSTE BOL VAN HET ATOMIUM (BEKEKEN VANUIT PALEIS 5)
PIETRO IS EEN TEVREDEN MAN.

Design: Clinton Stringer. **Title:** Dancing with an invisible partner. **Description:** A stop motion animation with Cynthia Loemij (Rosas) dancing with an 'invisible partner'. The 'partner' is made by cutting out a shape from each still and then re-photographing the stills. **School:** Sint-Lukas Brussels University College of Art & Design. **Country:** Belgium.

Design: Eszter Kapitany. **Title:** Subtown. **Description:** The book 'Subtown' is a work of fiction that tells a detective story set in an underground metro world. The protagonist is a heroic but introverted private detective called Peter Gocchi. The short novel, which shows a great attention for detail both in writing and illustration, mixes a sinister fantasy world with classic noir elements. In the seven chapters of the imaginary metro ride, Peter Gocchi meets evil little mice and other strange characters. The female protagonist is Helga, a rebel who is planning to blow up the artificial metro world of the GTA (Global Transit Authority). The happy ending, as well as the rest of the diploma thesis are accompanied by mixed technique illustrations that are very rich in detail. **School:** University of Applied Arts Vienna. **Country:** Austria.

GOCCHI quickly summing up the situation, runs up to the upper platform and throws himself down onto a train. He looses his balance for a moment, but regains it by grasping onto the ledge of the roof. Holding onto it, he tries to kick in one of the windows, but failing the first time, curses loudly.
THE third try proves successful. Kicking out the glass splinters, he climbs inside the car.

TRANSIT BAR
HEHE
AT the BAR where Gocchi is seated are three cocktail glasses: gin martinis. Two of them are empty; he sips from the third one. The smoke from his cigarette coils up into the air. Across from him, on the wall is a play of shadow and light from the passing subway cars. He drinks down his third drink and orders a fourth.

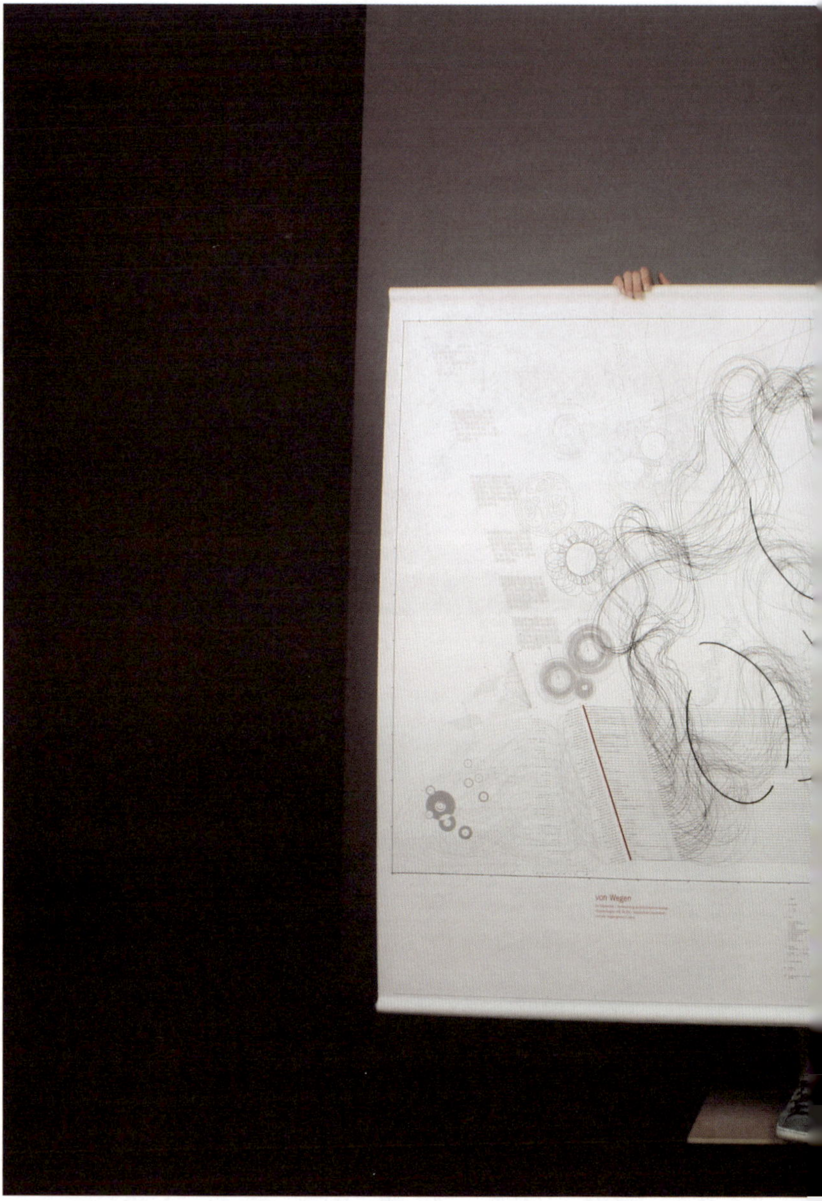
von Wegen

Design: Friederike Merkel. **Title:** von Wegen (about directions in life). **Description:** An information poster tracking hard and soft facts about private and university life of 30 students from start to finish of their student time, trying to illustrate personal and professional development and facts throughout that time and how they are related to each other. **School:** University of Applied Sciences Darmstadt. **Country:** Germany.

Design: Hélène Jacobs. **Title:** Avatar – 'Día de los muertos'. **Description:** This religiously inspired avatar is not digital. The basic character is inspired by the figure of the virgin Mary and consist of 3 layers, each one referring to the 7 sins. The user can mix the different sins in order to create newly combined sins. The graphical elements are inspired by the *'Día de los muertos'*, the Mexican celebration of the death. Catholic and original indian elements are brought together in surprising combinations. **School:** Sint-Lukas Brussels University College of Art & Design. **Country:** Belgium.

Design: Kees Peerdeman. **Title:** Isolation. **Description:** West-Friesian culture is highly reserved; the people in this region are not quick to talk about their qualms. Because of this, young people who are experiencing problems are especially vulnerable to becoming isolated. They will force themselves to keep their problems to themselves for fear of being seen as strange and becoming excluded from society. Many of them will suffer from depression, fear and anxiety complaints. Kees Peerdeman, born and raised in West-Friesland himself, has wanted to create more awareness around the fear of the unknown in the region and beyond it as well. He has collected his own experiences and put them into words and images in 'Isolation'; a graphic story. **School:** Design Academy Eindhoven. **Country:** The Netherlands.

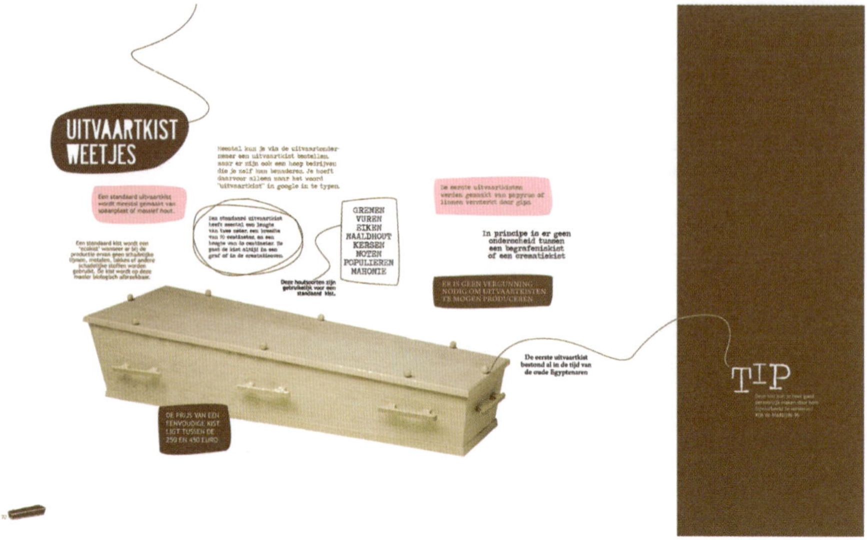

Design: Linda Korteland. **Title:** Doodleuk. **Description:** Death does not concern us; it is something we would rather not be confronted with. This is why we keep putting off the preparations for our own funeral. The result is often that relatives have to take a host of quick but difficult decisions during a very emotional time. With her activity book 'Doodleuk' Linda Korteland has wanted to give a clear and yet light-hearted overview of all the options surrounding a funeral. The book offers information, inspiration, and space to record your own ideas and wishes. This will make death a less difficult, and hopefully less frightening, subject to broach. More importantly, Doodleuk will comfort the bereaved and leave a tangible memory. **School:** Design Academy Eindhoven. **Country:** The Netherlands.

DOOD MAAR WAT DAN?

En dan is het opeens zo ver: je bent er niet meer. Wat dan? Vanaf nu volgt er een stappenplan die je helpt alle keuzes te maken die je tegen die tijd niet meer zal kunnen maken.

De keuzemogelijkheden worden op een luchtige manier voor je op een rijtje gezet. Je krijgt hier en daar informatie en doet inspiratie op voor het vormgeven van je uitvaart. Daarbij krijg je de ruimte om eigen ideeën toe te voegen en wensen vast te leggen. Zo ben je verrassend en actief bezig met het maken van jouw viering van je leven.

Design: Lucy Brooks. **Title:** Visual Biography. **Description:** Brief was to tell the biography of an individual visually using illustration as the main vehicle for communication. Subject chosen was Sylvia Plath. The resulting 24 page a pages book had 12 double-page spreads, which used the authors poems as captions to match the illustration to tell the story of Sylvia Plath's life. **School:** Nottingham Trent University. **Country:** United Kingdom.

But to others, this purpose meets their minds
Leaving no satisfaction. I need my father.

JULY

M	T	W	T	F	S	S
		1	2	3	4	5
6	7	8	9	10	11	12
13	14	15	16	17	18	19
20	21	22	23	24	25	26
27	28	29	30	31		

HIRE A BOAT IN LONDON

Regents Park, NW8
Battersea Park, SW11
Docklands Sailing Centre, E14
Putney Town Rowing Club, TW9

ADVENTURE CLOSE TO HOME

BEST PICNIC SPOTS

Hardcastle Crags, W Yorkshire
A deep, rocky ravine with tumbling streams and thick woods, the Crags is a great place for a walk and an exciting venue for a picnic. The easiest thing is to take the path down to the stream from the car park, and to eat at one of the picnic tables there before you walk.

Somerset House, London
If you're looking for somewhere to eat your sarnies in the middle of London, you won't find a better place than Somerset House. Perfect for an impromptu picnic - simply buy your provisions from one of the many sandwich shops, and then find a spot to sit down in the huge courtyard.

Tower Hill Tea Gardens, Kent
Walk along the seafront from Whitstable towards Tankerton and at the top of a steep slope you will find the Tea Gardens: beautifully kept lawns edged by herbaceous borders. It's a wonderfully relaxing spot with lovely views across the Thames estuary.

Forest of Dean Cycleway
Distance: a 12-mile route

The circular hard-packed track follows the former Severn and Wye Valley railway line, connecting former stations, old collieries, sculpture trails and some wonderful sections of the 27,000-acre deciduous and conifer forest.

Ramsgate to Deal
Distance: 13 miles one way

Follow the coastal path out of Ramsgate, through the fishing village of Cliffs End (a bird reserve) to the medieval town of Sandwich. History buffs can detour to Richborough Roman fort, thought to be the invasion beachhead in 43AD.

5 Four Castles Cycle Route
Distance: 32 miles

Out of Abergavenny and into the rolling Monmouthshire countryside, follow the route signs on B roads and delightful, quiet lanes, taking care not to get lost. All four Norman castles, built to defend the southern Marches and keep an eye on the Welsh, are wonderful.

THE BEST UK CYCLE ROUTES

theguardian

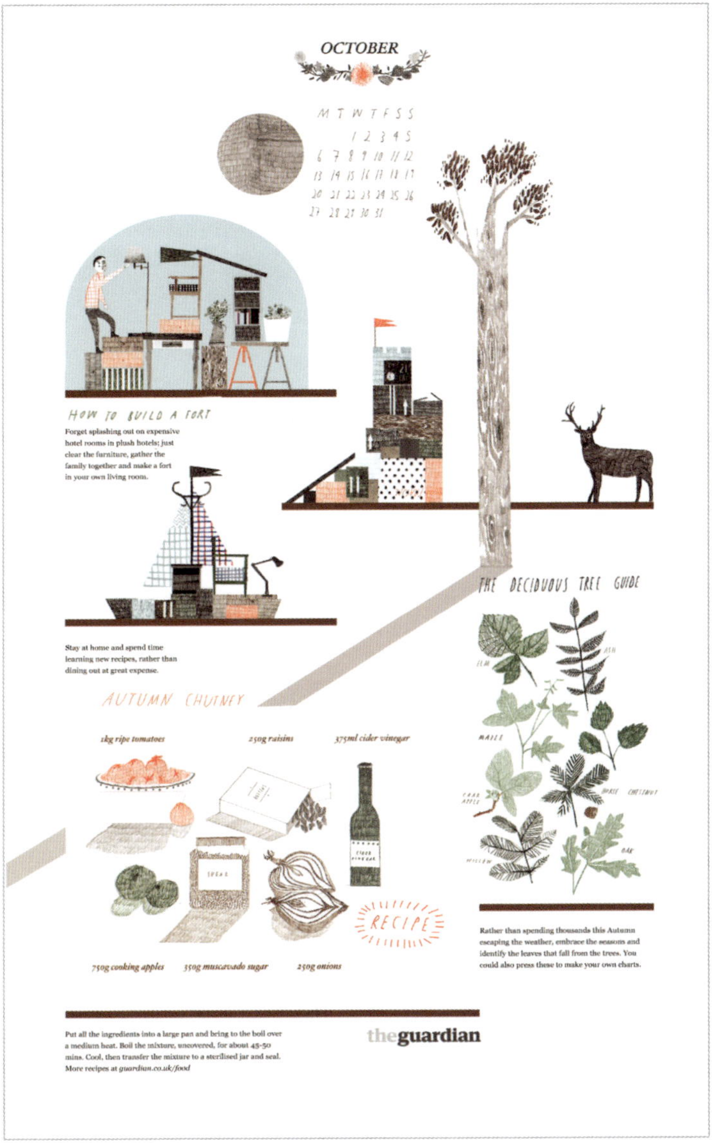

Design: Luke Fenech. **Title:** Staycation. **Description:** Posters designed to be sold with The Guardian newspaper that encourages its readers to holiday in Britain. By using the vast collective knowledge banks that The Guardian has, it displays information in a format that has more longevity and keepsake value the newspaper itself. By examining the typical activities one does on holiday, I can provide productive, practical British alternatives. **School:** Nottingham Trent University. **Country:** United Kingdom.

Design: Mª Reyes Guijarro Ruiz. **Title:** LuLLABY FOR THE APPLES OF MY EYES. **Description:** 'LuLLABY FOR THE APPLES OF MY EYES' is an illustrated book inspired by the british nonsense literature. It is a poem. A travel through a world without sense, at the borderland of dreams. It is a book to be read before sleep. **School:** Escuela de Arte 10. **Country:** Spain.

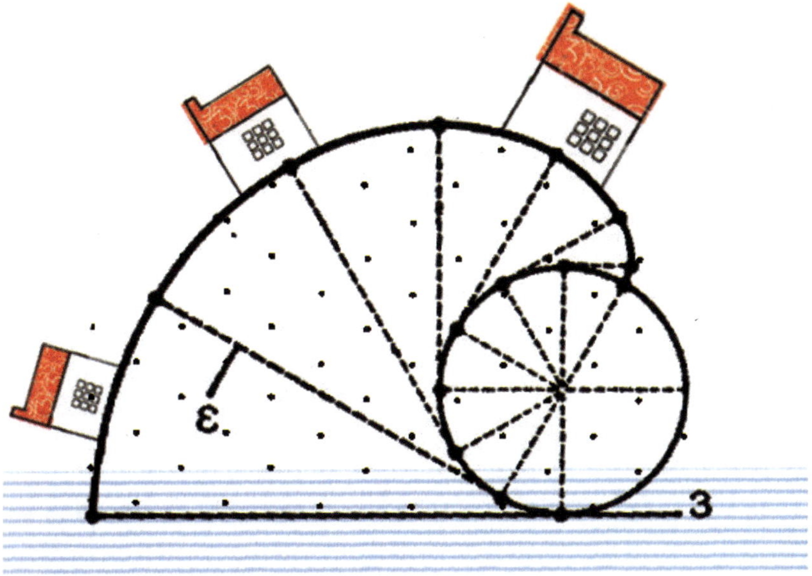

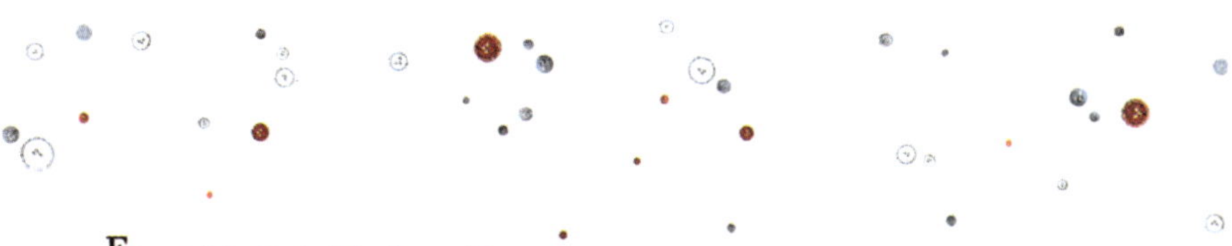

El secreto de las niñas de mis dos ojos encendidos.

Design: María Valle. **Title:** Puerto. **Description:** The idea of recuperating images related to maritime issues such as ports, their surroundings and activities involved is the starting point of this illustration project. The work is comprised of six illustration pieces that make up the word *'Puerto'* (port or harbour in Spanish). The intention is to encourage others to participate in the project by ways such as collecting or mailing the illustrations in question. **School:** IES La Albericia. **Country:** Spain.

T
O
Título_ "O" (5/5)
Medidas 15cms x 12,5 cms
Técnica Mixta
Esta tarjeta postal forma parte de una serie de cinco realizadas para la exposición "Ilustración & Comic"
Puerto de Santander
Junio/2009

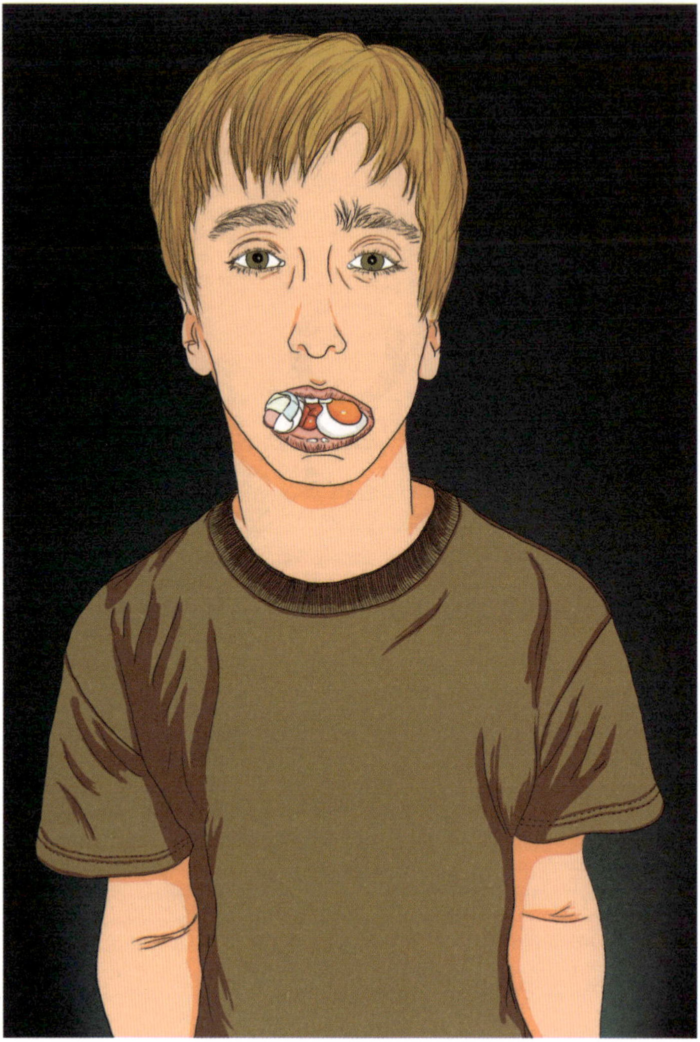

Design: Mónica Yang. **Title:** Hansel and Gretel. **Description:** 'Hansel and Gretel' was proposed for the UC – Project Illustration. I made two illustrations and chose two moments from this children's story. The first moment: 'Suddenly, in a clearing, they found a little house made of gingerbread and candy. The kids did not resist and they bite.' Here, it represents the only time that one of the children takes a bite at the house. I illustrated just one of the children with a mouth of jelly gums as if he'd just pulled the jelly gums and the house and was eating them. The second moment: '... Hansel was closed inside a cage with the intent to fatten him.' In this excerpt I drew the state in which Hansel is found inside the cage. Sitting at the bottom of Darkness (for the cage does not let him move to any place, being enclosed and sad), his head rests on his arms, which rest on his knees, showing the desperation, which feels like being inside the cage. **School:** IADE – Creative University (Escola Superior de Design). **Country:** Portugal.

Design: Sara Costantini. **Title:** 'Pezzettini'. **Description:** In *'Pezzettini'* (Shreds of Me) the artist uses drawings of the nursery and constructs a dialogue with herself to explain who she is now, thanks to who she was then. **School:** Escola d'Art i Superior de Disseny Pau Gargallo. **Country:** Spain.

MAMMA A VOLTE PROVA A FARE I DOLCI. SE ESCONO MALE LI DÀ ALLE GALLINE. CHE NON MI FACEVANO PAURA: UN GIORNO PERÒ HO MESSO IL DITO NELLA RETE DEL POLLAIO. QUELLE SCEME L'HANNO SCAMBIATO PER UNA CAROTA E MI HANNO BECCATO. DA ALLORA, SE LE VEDO SCAPPO.

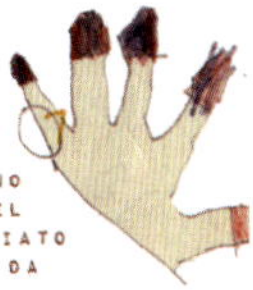

Design: Zé Burnay. **Title:** Woods. **Description:** My objective in this illustration was to create an enigmatic and strong image, inspired by sci-fi and horror movies from the 50's. **School:** Escola Superior de Artes e Design de Caldas da Rainha. **Country:** Portugal.

zé BURNAY

New Media

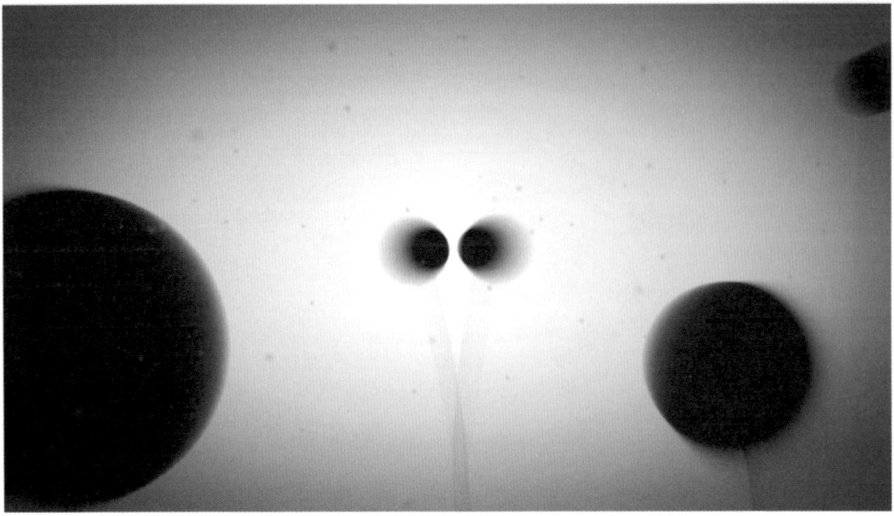

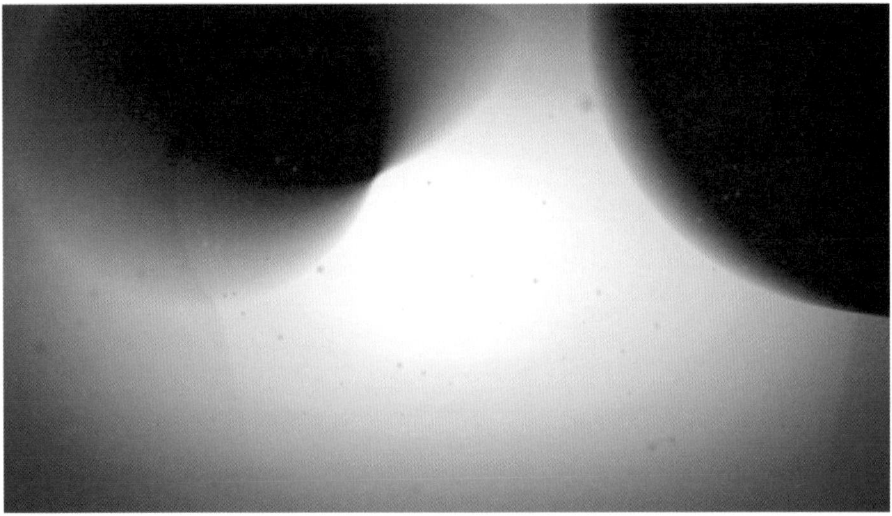

Design: Alba Díaz, José Vanaclocha. **Title:** Museo Thyssen-Bornemisza / EducaThyssen. **Description:** Opening title sequence for the audiovisual material of the Thyssen-Bornemisza Museum and their educational area EducaThyssen. Based on nature's live elements as a basis for art, and comparing it with it's growth through the years. **School:** Istituto Europeo di Design IED, Madrid. **Country:** Spain.

DVD

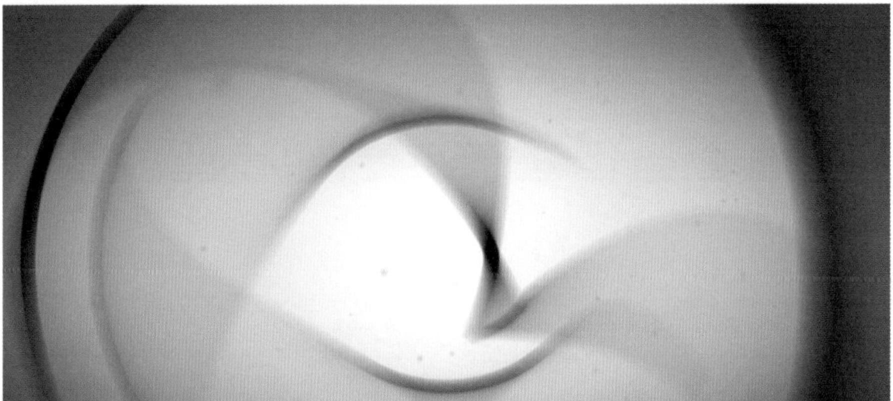

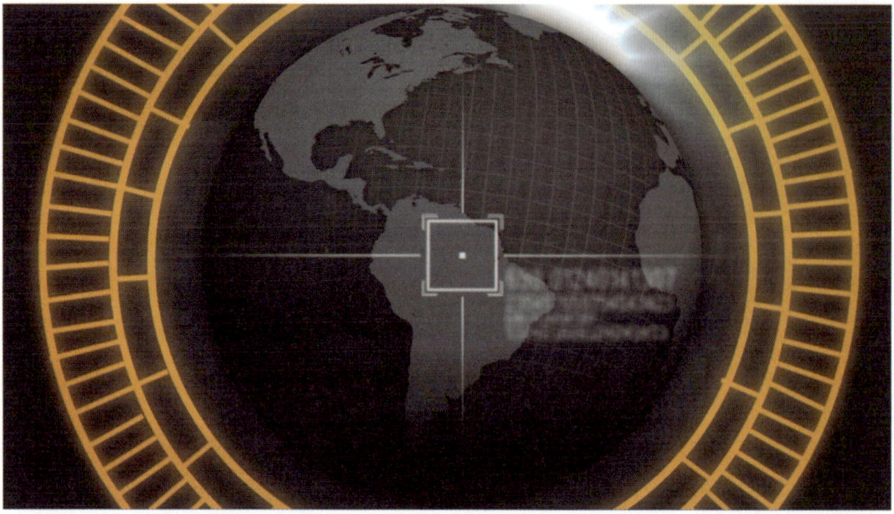

Design: Ambrogio Moretti, Fabio Meliffi, Giulia Palladini, Lara Sabattini, Mattia Lopriore. **Title:** J.A.S.T. **Description:** Realization of a promotional book trailer for the release of the book JAST by Lorenza Ghinelli, Daniel Rudolph, Simone Sarasso, published by Marsilio Editori, Italy. The spy novel that will revolutionize the genre is presented through eye-catching graphics and a pressing edit. Something very dangerous is stolen from a military base of the U.S. government. The four secret agents who follow the trail of the mysterious object are presented through detailed technical dossiers. Aisha, a CIA agent, Dekhnavitsh Mordechai, the number one of Mossad and Viscardi, the ruthless Vatican murderer are chasing the Spy, the man with no name, who stole what could change the fate of the planet. **School:** NABA Nuova Accademia di Belle Arti Milano. **Country:** Italy.

//ISRAELE//
488.150312810775
-45.3427028707721
15:30
GPRS
LUOGO ISRAELE
NOME Mordechai
SERVIZI SEGRETI
MOSSAD

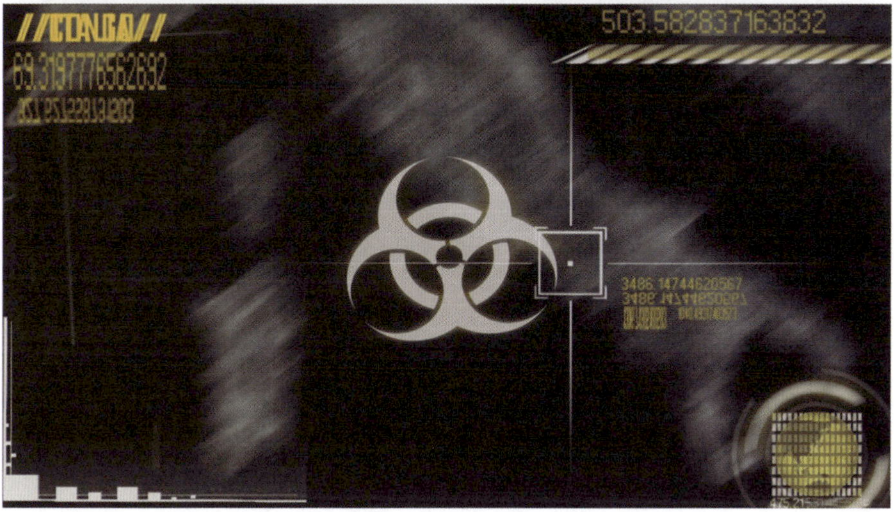
503.582837163832
69.3197776562692
3486.14744620567

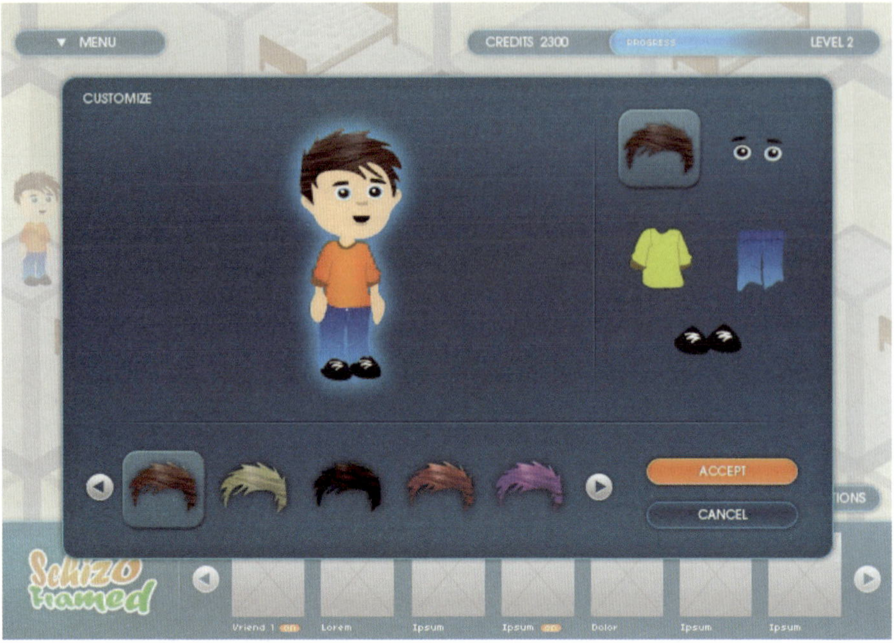
MENU
CREDITS 2300
PROGRESS
LEVEL 2
CUSTOMIZE
ACCEPT
CANCEL
Vriend 1
Lorem
Ipsum
Ipsum
Dolor
Ipsum
Ipsum

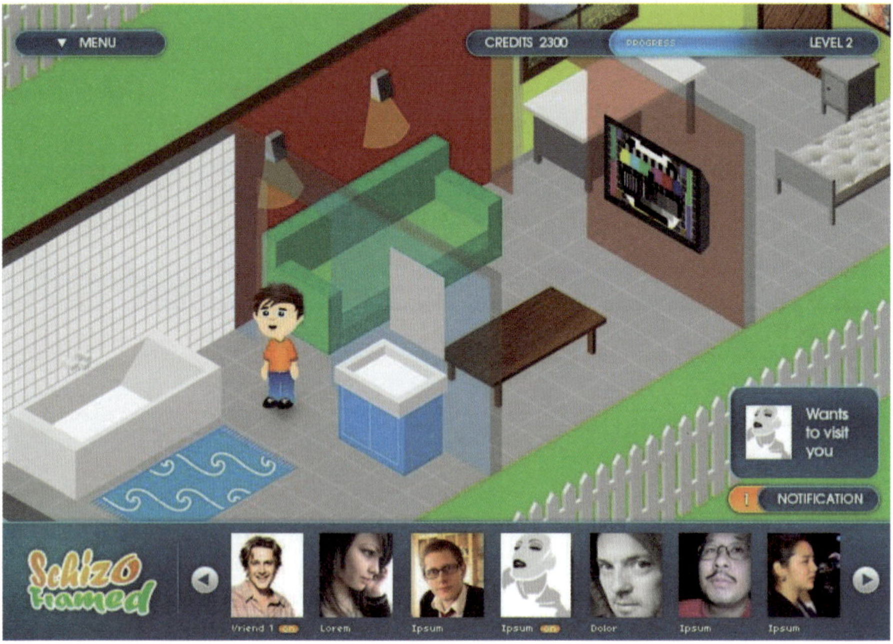
MENU
CREDITS 2300
PROGRESS
LEVEL 2
Wants to visit you
1 NOTIFICATION
Vriend 1
Lorem
Ipsum
Ipsum
Dolor
Ipsum
Ipsum

Design: Ben Marckx, Cindy Paesen, Nicky Steegmans, Seppe Janssen, Wim Bussels, Wouter Medaer. **Title:** Schizofrenia. **Description:** The target group are patients with schizophrenia. Students are seeking solutions through specific design research methods to come closer to the target group. They design from this study possibilities to improve the environment of the patients or the public perception of schizofrenia. **School:** MAD-Faculty. **Country:** Belgium.

Design: Joan Martín Giménez. **Title:** 'El Vespre'. **Description:** This project is an animated short. Technique is performed with Stop Motion and lasts for five minutes. It is the story of a man who believes that life has nothing to offer and prepares to wrap up. **School:** Escola d'Art i Superior de Disseny Pau Gargallo. **Country:** Spain.

sound

ears

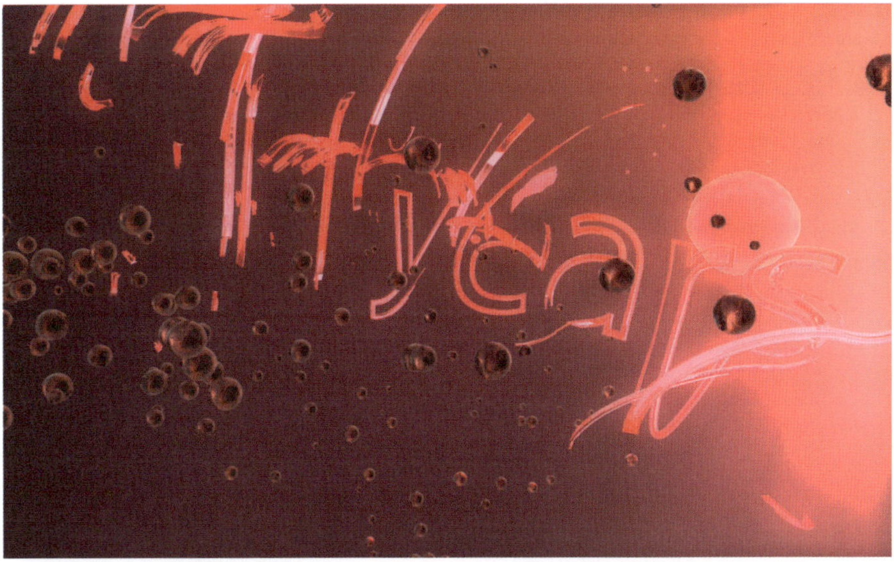

Design: Luke Busby. **Title:** Visualising Sound. **Description:** Using typography, visualise a piece of poetry, prose or lyrics from a song. The song chosen was 'What Sound' by Lamb. **School:** Nottingham Trent University. **Country:** United Kingdom.

Design: Naomi Yasuda. **Title:** Luisterlandschap. **Description:** Google Maps has brought an incredible amount of images of the world within reach, which is great, but I miss the interaction. Auditory impressions will be a major factor in determining our experience. In *'Luisterlandschap'* I made Google Maps come to life by adding sound. My first voyage of discovery is the Pieterpad, a walk that runs from the Pieterburen village in Northern Groningen to the Sint-Pietersberg hill in the South of Limburg. Through www.luisterlandschap.nl anyone can travel along with me. Scroll over the walkway, add sounds and comments where needed, and experience a new way of travelling. **School:** Design Academy Eindhoven. **Country:** The Netherlands.

Luisterlandschap

Design: Zlaten del Castillo. **Title:** Ran. **Description:** This is an alternative opening title sequence for 'Ran' from film director Akira Kurosawa. The combination of three colours represent each act within the film. To symbolise the cruelty of a battle, fast movements mark each sequence. **School:** Istituto Europeo di Design IED, Madrid. **Country:** Spain.

TOSHIYA ITÖ

Packaging

Design: Albert Martínez. **Title:** The Selin Tools. **Description:** The proposed brief was to develop a line of packaging for a tools company. The objective was to realize an image that differentiates the brand and explains the use of the tools through interaction between the object and the packaging. **School:** IDEP Institut Superior de Disseny. **Country:** Spain.

SELIN
VERKTYG
VÄXTER JORD
25KG.

Design: Cristina Hernández Navarro. **Title:** FUNNY! A Juvenile Line of Erotic Toys. **Description:** The purpose of this project is to launch a new line of sex toys designed for a younger demographic and to encourage a new way of understanding sex. In recent years, we have observed a very powerful cultural change in sex education, especially by younger generations. This shift demands a change in how we see and design these products. The younger public needs, above all, a brand that reflects power, which is enjoyable and attractive, and that speaks their language, treating them on equal terms with a close and casual language. The most important goal is to remove the taboo that still exists with sex education and make them clearly understand the following: 'SEX IS SOMETHING VERY FUNNY, ALONE, OR IN COMPANY'. **School:** Escuela Superior de Diseño Región de Murcia. **Country:** Spain.

funny!
Oh YESSSSSSSSS
sex
mmm...
100%
SILICONA
FUNNY!

funny!
funny!
funny!
YES YES YESSSSS YES
yesss!
FUNNY!

PREMIUM · CERVESA
MORITZ
1856
BARCELONA

Design: Francisco Lopéz, Polina Raevskaya. **Title:** Moritz Premium Beer. **Description:** This packaging project is for Moritz Premium Beer. When several six-packs are assembled together, they form the ornament of the Eixample district of Barcelona, which is a symbol of the city as well as the Moritz Beer. **School:** Istituto Europeo di Design, IED Barcelona. **Country:** Spain.

Design: Hans Zoons. **Title:** Non-Subjective Design. **Description:** The 'fourth wall' is a term used in the theater. It breaks the experience of a theater or movie by directly engaging the audience. This concept was used in packaging. What happens when we remove emotion from packaging and keep only the functionality? This was a complex study in which every subjective decision of the designer was removed. The acronym with its positive and negative images determine the grid and placement. Each brand gets its own grid in this way, its own system. **School:** MAD-Faculty. **Country:** Belgium.

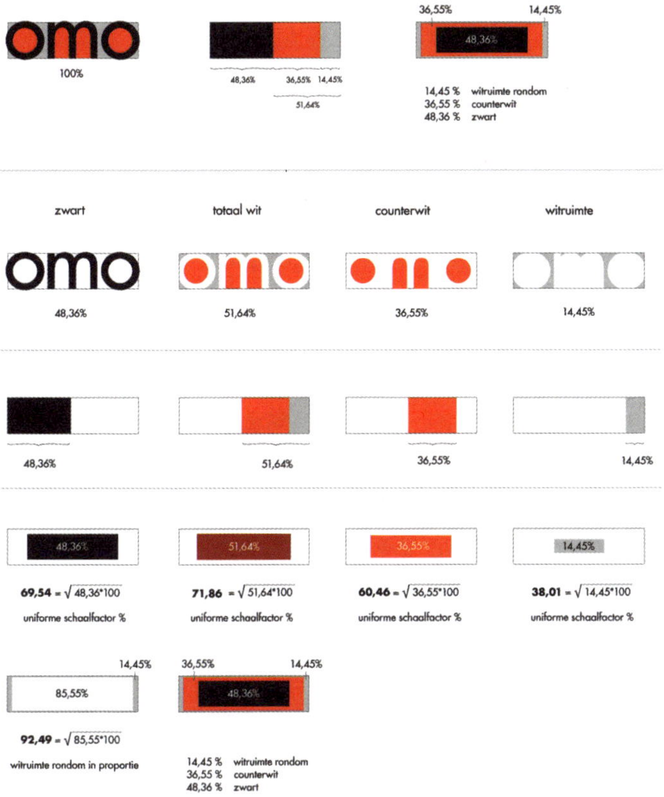

berekenen percentage vlak binnen vlak, binnen de methode Zoons

47 weten we, is het gewenste percentage van het vlak, binnen het groter vlak

x moeten we weten, is de "uniforme procentualiteit" van het vak (dat heb ik uitgevonden)

met andere woorden, met hoeveel x moeten we schalen zodat het gekleurd vak 47% grootte heeft van het groter vak?

$$\frac{x * x}{100} = 47$$

$$x * x = 47 * 100$$

$$x^2 = 47 * 100$$

$$x = \sqrt{47 * 100}$$

$$\mathbf{68.55} = \sqrt{47} * 100$$

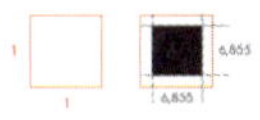

$$\frac{6,855 * 6,855}{1} = 47$$

Posters

Design: Agnes Steiner. **Title:** Grafische Revue. **Description:** *'Grafische Revue'* is the title of both the poster and the lecture by Grafisches Büro. This title is charged with a certain poetry, which I have attempted to sustain in my poster. In my opinion, compounding the French term *vue* (seeing, view, sight, vision) – be it *entrevue* (meeting), *à vue* (at sight), *revue* (review, magazine), *bévue* (blunder, mistake), *en vue* (coveted, in sight), *prevue* (planned), *longue vue* (telescope), *point de vue* (point of view, perspective) or *double vue* (second sight, clairvoyance) – opens up interpretation for the context of graphic design and our work in this field. At first sight, the poster may appear raw, as the concept of antidesign might be interpreted as well. In reality, however, it is the result of a graphic process that seems to be coincidental rather than reflecting a rejection of design. Quite the contrary, the poster is carefully planned and realised with great attention to detail regarding both its typography and its composition. **School:** University of Applied Arts Vienna. **Country:** Austria.

VUE
POINT DE VUE
ENTREVUE
LONGUE VUE
KLASSE FÜR GRAFIKDESIGN, PROF. OLIVER KARTAK
À VUE
Grafische REVUE
MI, 17. JUNI, 2009, 19.00 UHR
DIPLOMAUSSTELLUNG: NATALIE DIETRICH ANNA KASNYIK YANYAN LI 17.–19. JUNI 2009
DOUBLE VUE
VORTRAG
GRAFISCHES BÜRO GÜNTER EDER, ROMAN BREIER, MARCEL NEUNDÖRFER
BÉVUE
www.g-b.at
PREVUE
EN VUE
AB, DACHGESCHOSS
SEMINARRAUM B, UNIVERSITÄT FÜR ANGEWANDTE KUNST

Design: Afonso Arraiano. **Title:** Blade Runner. **Description:** The poster uses the Blade Runner movie as a point of departure to show the ambiguous and sometimes antagonic relationships between man and machine. By 'humanising' the machine, I tried to narrow the gap. The concept was developed by using only one geometric form, the triangle, which repeats itself in order to suggest a symbiosis between its digital and futurist pattern in addition to the white dove, a symbol that serves as both an icon and a bridge from past to future. **School:** Escola Superior de Artes e Design de Caldas da Rainha. **Country:** Portugal.

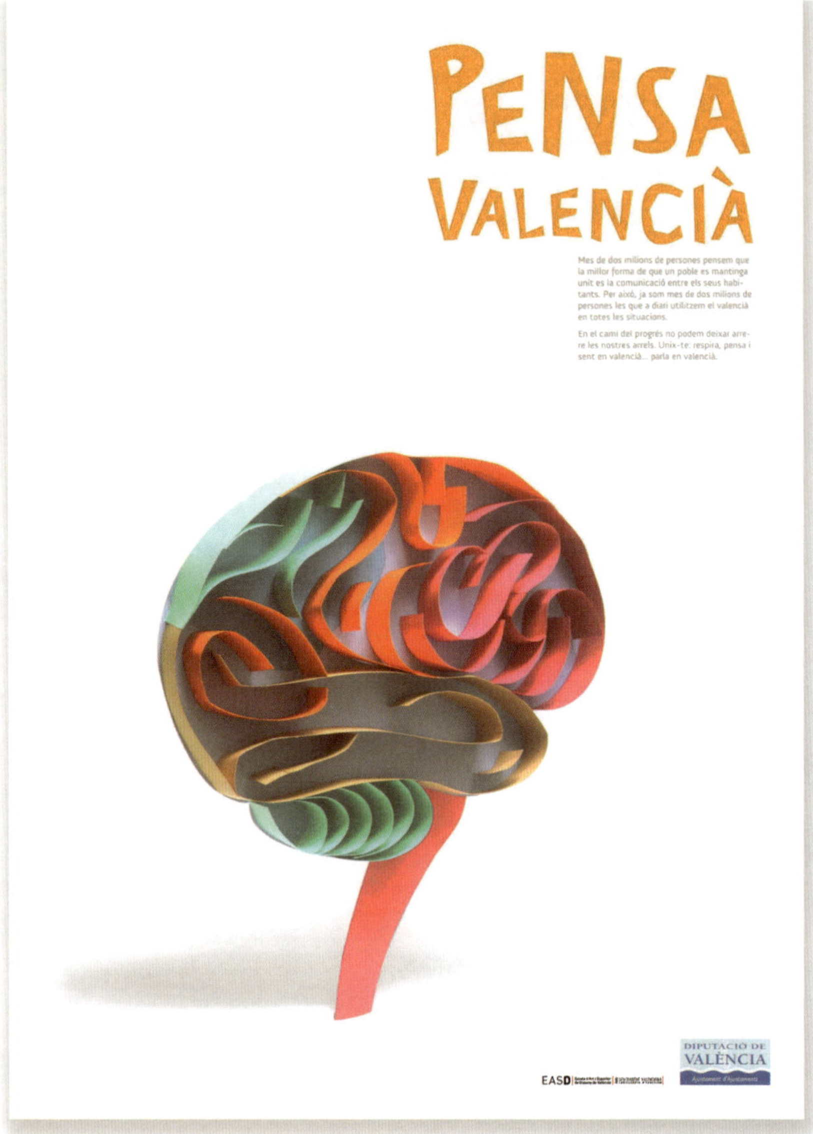

PENSA VALENCIÀ
Mes de dos milions de persones pensem que la millor forma de que un poble es mantinga unit es la comunicació entre els seus habitants. Per això, ja som mes de dos milions de persones les que a diari utilitzem el valencià en totes les situacions.
En el camí del progrés no podem deixar arrere les nostres arrels. Unix-te: respira, pensa i sent en valencià... parla en valencià.
EASD
DIPUTACIÓ DE VALÈNCIA

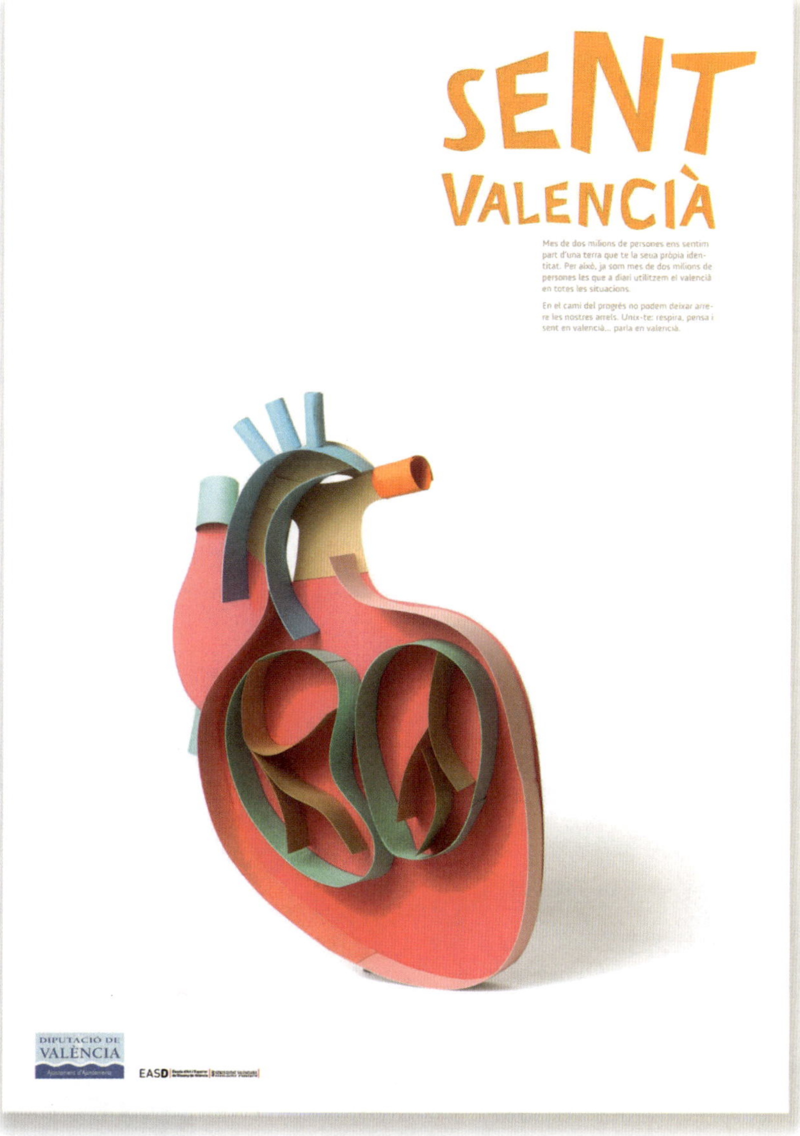

Design: Cristina Jaramago. Photography: Marcos Valdés. **Title:** Campaña Diputación. **Description:** Made to promote the use of the Valencian language, captures the attention through handmade cardboard organs whose function is vital. The slogan campaign is *Siente valenciano, piensa valenciano, respira valenciano*, it means that feel, think and breathe Valencian language is a good way for living. Campaign elements of promotion: stickers (for trains and cars), stamper, pens and rubber bracelets, pocket calendars and notebooks. **School:** Escuela de Arte y Superior de Diseño de Valencia. **Country:** Spain.

Design: Nahuel Marín Luriaud. **Title:** X Conference on Design Film and TV. **Description:** These posters were created for the X Conference on Design of the ESD of Murcia. This year, the theme was design applied to movies and television. A series of six posters of different geometric typography were developed to break into the background. **School:** Escuela Superior de Diseño Región de Murcia. **Country:** Spain.

X Jornadas
de Diseño — *Cine* y *TV*
EASD de Murcia

Design: Tina Michl. **Title:** Show Down (poster). **Description:** 'Show Down' promotes a one-day exhibition held 5 May 2010 from 12:00 to 24:00 with installations, videos, performances, etc., on the theme of conflicting opinions within design and in general at the Darmstadt University of Applied Sciences, Faculty of Design. **School:** University of Applied Sciences Darmstadt. **Country:** Germany.

12
STUNDEN
SHOWDOWN
IM
KONFLIKT

Promotions

Design: Elena Luongo. **Title:** BIC – Long Writing. **Description:** The advertising was developed as an academic exercise. The purpose was to highlight one of the primary product's features, for example, the longevity of the BIC pen. The visual treatment can have an immediate impact but at the same time can be very simple. The idea is based on a picture that clearly demonstrates the quality of the pen. **School:** NABA Nuova Accademia di Belle Arti Milano. **Country:** Italy.

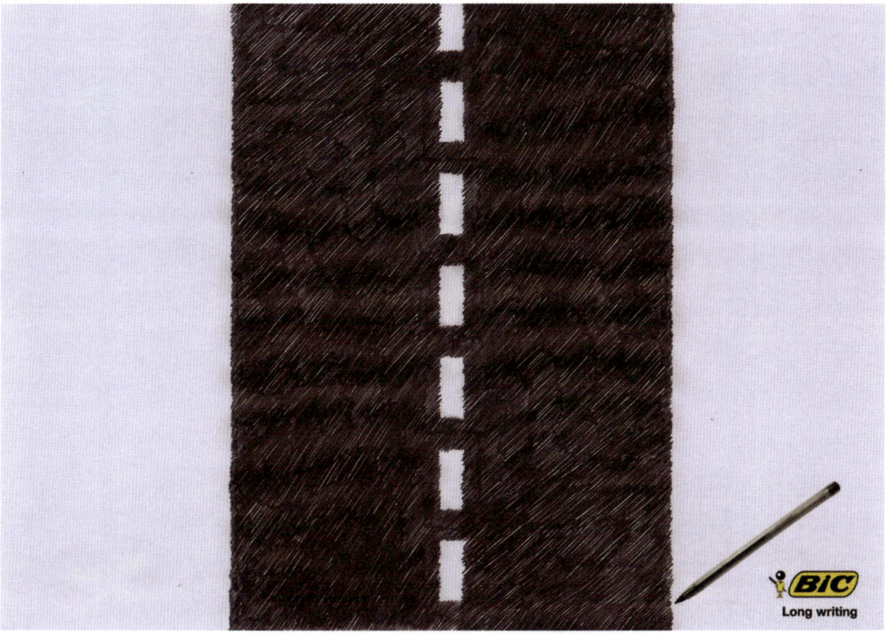
BIC
Long writing

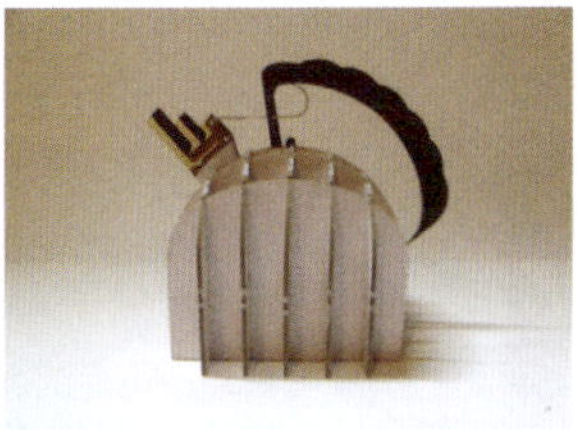

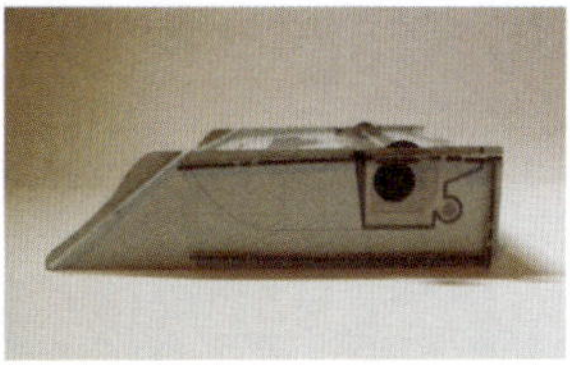

Design: Laura Quantril. **Title:** Fedrigoni. **Description:** Fedrigoni are part of the century old tradition of Italian paper making and throughout the years their stocks have become a part of Italian design culture and heritage. Fedrigoni are classic Italian design in their own right and to celebrate them I've created a mailer to promote an exhibition of classic Italian design throughout the 20th century at the Fedrigoni London showroom. Life-sized paper representations of timeless Italian design will be included; in order to whet clients' appetites, Fedrigoni paper models of Italian design classics will be sent out, which allow studios to sample the range of stocks with a Vespa, Sapper Alessi kettle and Olivetti typewriter models. Designers will also be invited to create their own paper representations of classic Italian design to bring to the exhibition event. **School:** Nottingham Trent University. **Country:** United Kingdom.

Design: Marc Sancho. **Title:** Ai not andernsteniu. **Description:** My proposal is based on the creation of a festival where the basic premise is not to know how to sing in English, but want to sing it regardless. The whole graphic for the event is created around this concept, which is reinforced with the inclusion of popular recording artists who have sung in English but in their own very particular way, for example, Raphael, Josmar, Príncipe Gitano, Julio Iglesias, etc. **School:** IDEP Institut Superior de Disseny. **Country:** Spain.

AI NOT ANDERN STENIU
Festival de música avanzada para gente que no sabe inglés pero quiere cantar en inglés
del 21.12 al 22.12
ai not ander steniu
ai not ander steniu
wachins fonder nau?

Oh! mai lovi!

www.ingravitt.com

Design: Marina Candeal. **Title:** Ingravitt. **Description:** This corporate identity was designed for a school of dance and body disciplines. **School:** BAU, Escola Superior de Disseny. **Country:** Spain.

Design: Sónia Morgado. **Title:** Pop-Up Flyer 'Falo Fest'. **Description:** The presented project *'Falo Fest'* was created in order to promote an event titled Caldas da Rainha World Capital of the Penis. This project was rooted in the typical ceramics of Caldas da Rainha and their mischief as well as the organic framework of the pottery and floral themes of the region. The choice of the word *phallo* (in Portuguese, *falo*), rather than the word penis, was best because it is more figurative and symbolic. For example, *phallo* is usually defined as the symbolic representation of the erect penis, which is the characteristic figure of the town. Therefore, Caldas da Rainha Phallo Fest was the concept and the goal was to announce an event that would be a party, making a connection with the word mischief and the playfulness of Caldas da Rainha. **School:** Escola Superior de Artes e Design de Caldas da Rainha. **Country:** Portugal.

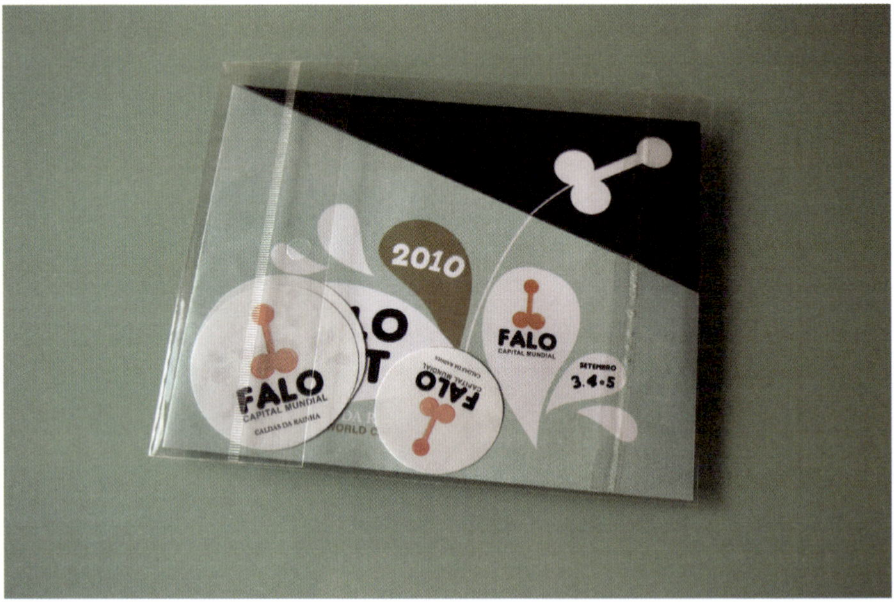

CONCERTOS
CONCERTS
ENTRADAS GRATUITAS
FREE PASS
EXPOSIÇÕES
EXHIBITIONS
2010
ANIMAÇÕES
ANIMATIONS
FALO
CAPITAL MUNDIAL
falo
phallo
Sep.

2010
FALO
CAPITAL MUNDIAL

TEA & BISCUITS

The Fedrigoni Showroom,

a place to feel at home.

Design: Toby Edwards. **Title:** Fedrigoni. **Description:** The brief of the Young Creative Network competition was to promote the Fedrigoni Paper Showroom to designers. Using the event theme of 'Tea and Biscuits', the idea was to encourage creatives to feel more at home at Fedrigoni. The logo makes use of 1930's Italian typographic style and a decagon form, which was inspired by the shape of old biscuit tins. I created a giant teapot installation using a range of Fedrigoni paper stocks. The teapot serves as a showpiece to attract visitors to the showroom while at the same time displaying the many paper stocks that Fedrigoni produces. **School:** Nottingham Trent University. **Country:** United Kingdom.

Typography

Design: Alex Fowkes. **Title:** Fedrigoni. **Description:** The aim of the Young Creative Network competition was to promote the Fedrigoni Paper Showroom to designers. The concept was to develop an event based around the recent documentary on woodcut type called Typeface by Justine Nagan. Along with screenings of the film during the weekend, there were letterpress machines for attendants to print their own limited edition Fedrigoni postcards, allowing attendants to select colour, the chase, and stock from a range of Fedrigoni papers. **School:** Nottingham Trent University. **Country:** United Kingdom.

FEDRIGONI PRESENTS
A PLACE FOR LETTER PRESS
A WEEKEND OF TRADITIONAL TYPE & FILM
MAY 22-23 10 AM TILL 6 PM
INCLUDING SCREENINGS OF
THE CRITICALLY ACCLAIMED DOCUMENTARY
TYPE FACE
A FILM BY JUSTINE NAGAN
SCREENINGS 12PM AND 3PM
FEDRIGONI LONDON SHOWROOM
5th FLOOR DIAMOND HOUSE
36-38 HATTON GARDEN
LONDON EC1N 8EB
WWW.APLACEFORLETTERPRESS.COM

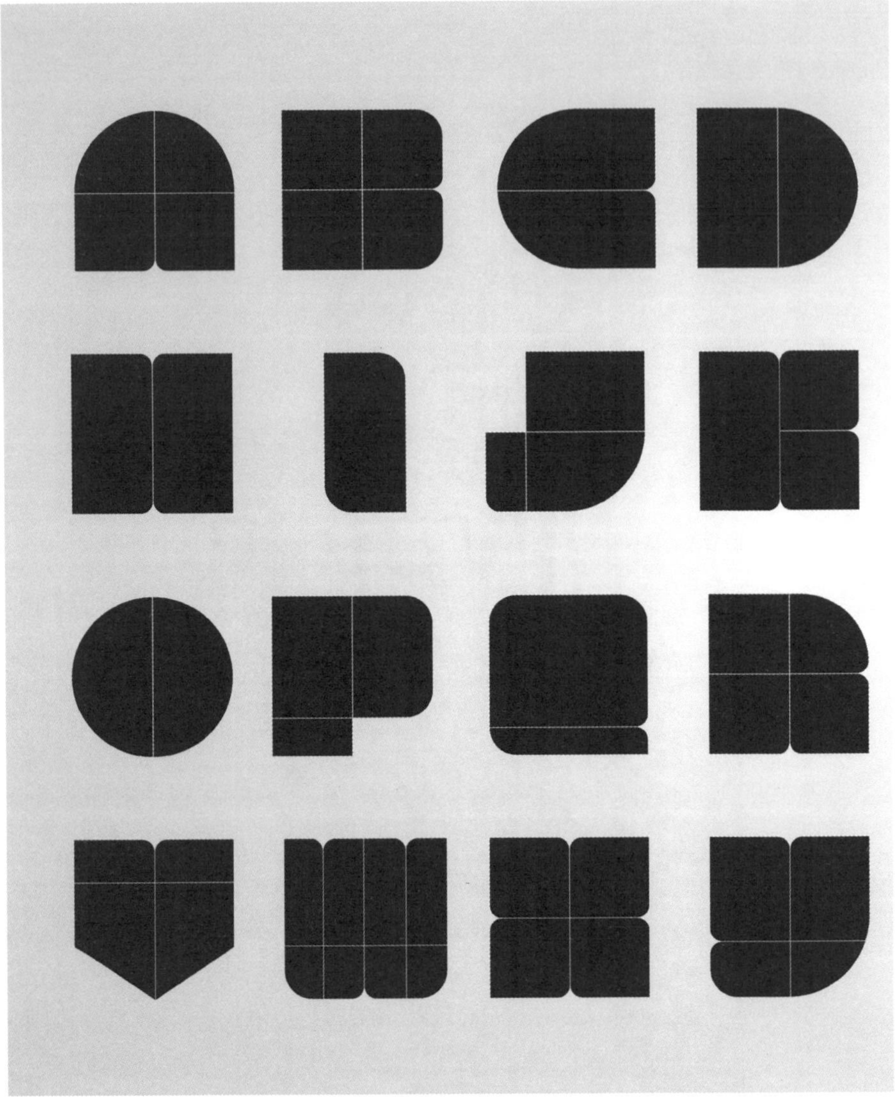

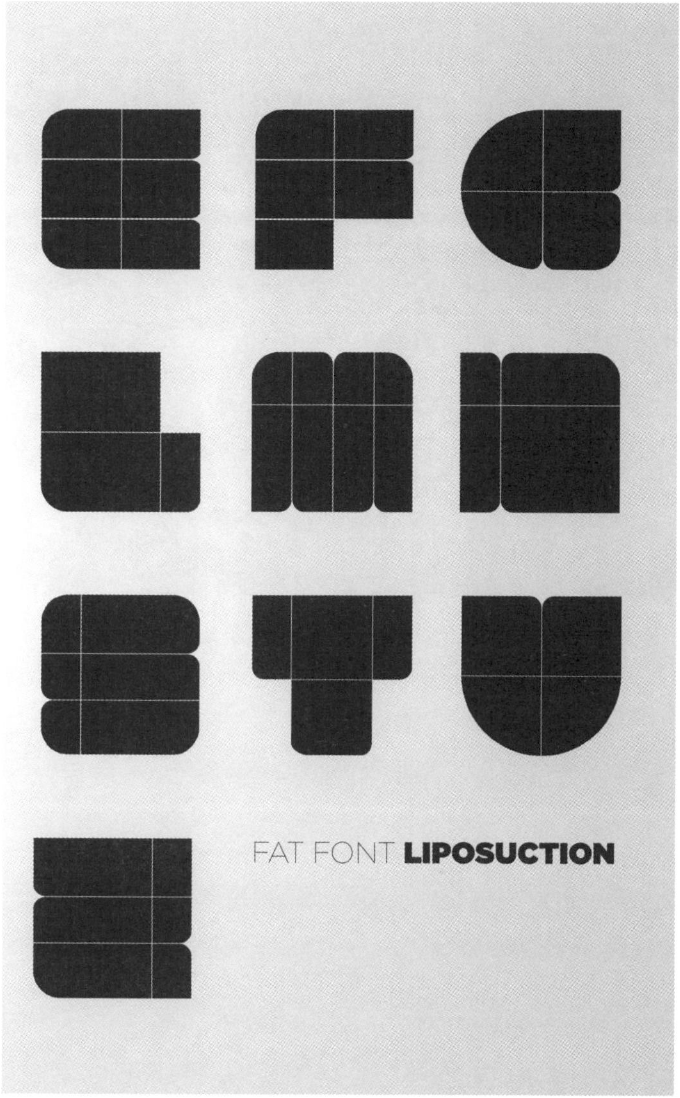

Design: Christian El Asmar. **Title:** Liposuction. **Description:** We start with a fat, black square. We cut it, trim it, take out the fat and model it until forms start to appear. The result is this typography, the name of which explains the process of its creation. **School:** Miami Ad School Madrid. **Country:** Spain.

Design: Clinton Stringer. **Title:** Cuneiform Roman. **Description:** The starting point for this typeface design was the theme 'source'. The source of all alphabets comes from the Sumerians with their cuneiform alphabet. I took the basic wedge-shape, which originated from the end of a reed, and created a pattern. This pattern I used as a basis for creating an upper-case Roman alphabet. The typeface was used in the signage for the end-of-year exhibition of Sint-Lukas Brussels University College of Art and Design, 2010. **School:** Sint-Lukas Brussels University College of Art and Design. **Country:** Belgium.

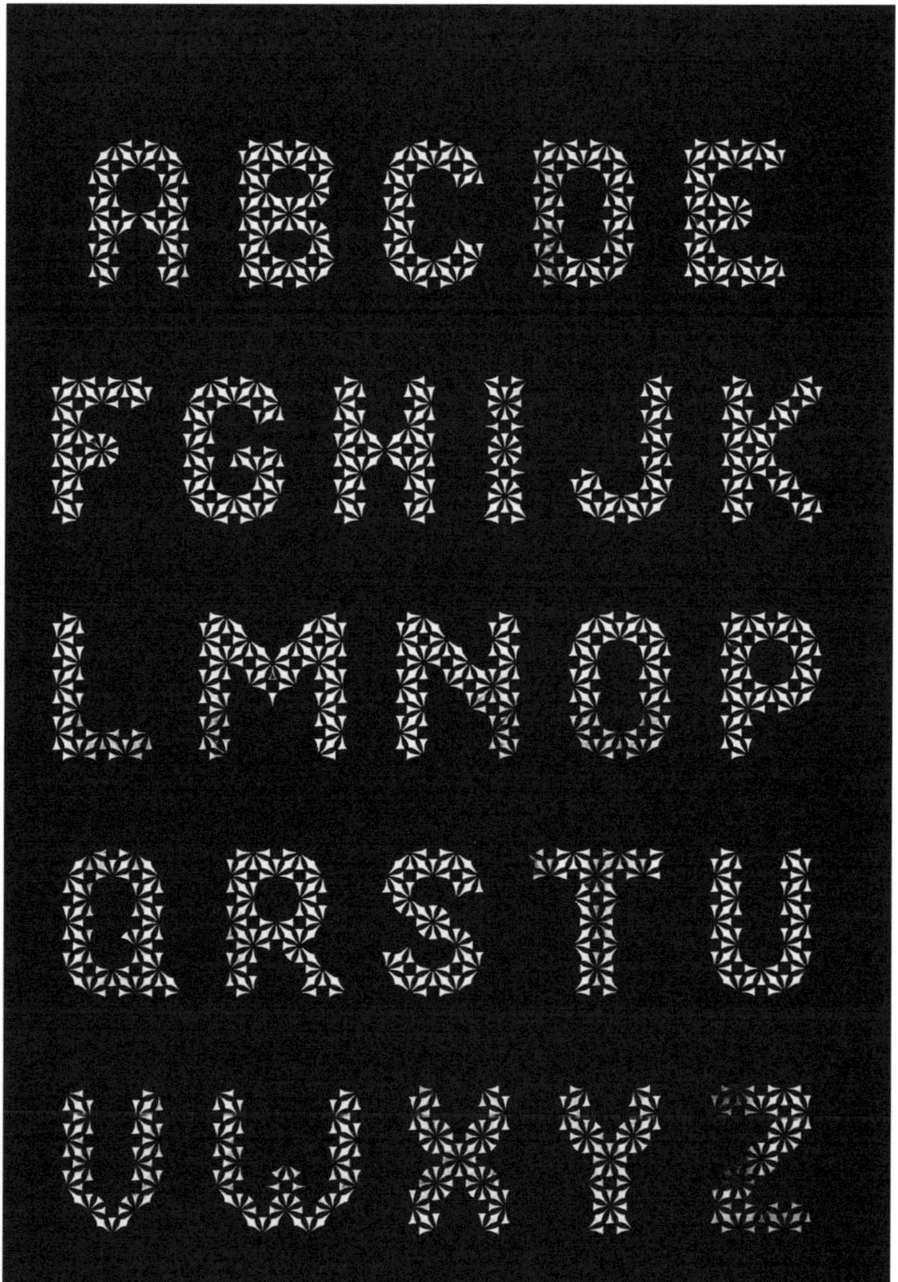
ABCDE
FGHIJK
LMNOP
QRSTU
VWXYZ

Design: Inge Van Ginderachter. **Title:** Mendeljev. **Description:** This is an accordion book with a historical overview of the elements of the periodic table. After reading the book, you can rip off each element and arrange it like the periodic table by using an indication system. **School:** Sint-Lukas Brussels University College of Art and Design. **Country:** Belgium.

Yb
Rb
Ru
Er
V
Al
Si
Li

Directory

A

Academy of Fine Arts and Design 32
dekanat@aluo.uni-lj.si – www.aluo.uni-lj.si – Slovenia

B

BAU Escola Superior de Disseny 50, 62, 188
info@baued.es – www.baued.es – Spain

D

Design Academy Eindhoven 100, 124, 126, 154
info@designacademy.nl – www.designacademy.nl – The Netherlands

E

Eina, Escola de Disseny i Art 38, 42, 88
info@eina.edu – www.eina.edu – Spain

ELISAVA Escola Superior de Disseny i Enginyeria de Barcelona 64, 82, 96
comunicacio@elisava.net – www.elisava.net – Spain

Escola d'Art i Superior de Disseny Pau Gargallo 138, 150
escola@paugargallo.net – www.paugargallo.net – Spain

Escola Superior de Artes e Design de Caldas da Rainha 16, 112, 140, 172, 190
esad@esad.ipleiria.pt – www.esad.ipleiria.pt – Portugal

Escuela de Arte 10 132
escuela@artediez.es – www.artediez.es – Spain

Escuela de Arte y Superior de Diseño Valencia 26, 28, 80, 98, 174
grafico@easdvalencia.com – www.easdvalencia.com – Spain

Escuela Superior de Diseño Región de Murcia 34, 60, 92, 162, 176
esdmurciapromocion@gmail.com – www.easdmurcia.es – Spain

I

IADE – Creative University (Escola Superior de Design) 22, 136
iade@iade.pt – www.iade.pt – Portugal

IDEP Institut Superior de Disseny 54, 84, 86, 160, 186
info@idep.es – www.idep.es – Spain

IES La Albericia 134
correo@iesalbericia.com – www.iesalbericia.com – Spain

Istituto Europeo di Design, IED Barcelona 164
comunicacion@bcn.ied.es – www.iedbarcelona.es – Spain

Istituto Europeo di Design, IED Madrid 70, 144, 156
info@madrid.ied.es – www.iedmadrid.com – Spain

K

Köln International School of Design 40
c.moritz@kisd.de – www.kisd.de – Germany

M

MAD-Faculty 46, 148, 166
info@mda.khlim.be – www.mad-fac.be – Belgium

Miami Ad School Madrid 198
infomd@miamiadschool.com – www.miamiadschool.es – Spain

N

NABA Nuova Accademia di Belle Arti Milano **146, 182**
comunicazione@naba.it – www.naba.it – Italy

Nottingham Trent University **36, 78, 90, 128, 130, 152, 184, 192, 196**
ntsad@ntu.ac.uk – www.ntu.ac.uk – United Kingdom

S

Sint-Lukas Brussels University College of Art & Design **68, 72, 74, 76, 114,**
inge.gobert@sintlukas.be – www.sintlukas.be – Belgium **116, 122, 200, 202**

U

University of Applied Arts Vienna **44, 52, 94, 118, 170**
mail@klassekartak.com – www.klassekartak.com – Austria

University of Applied Sciences Darmstadt **14, 56, 58, 66, 102, 106, 120, 178**
frank.philippin@h-da.de – www.fbg.h-da.de – Germany

W

Willem de Kooning Academy **18, 20, 24, 108**
r.teeuwen@hro.nl – www.wdka.nl – The Netherlands

Call for entries for Selected C

www.indexbook.com/selected/